The
Holy
Spirit

THE WESLEYAN THEOLOGY SERIES

The Holy Spirit

Frank Moore

f

THE FOUNDRY
PUBLISHING

Copyright © 2023 by Frank Moore

The Foundry Publishing®
PO Box 419527
Kansas City, MO 64141
thefoundrypublishing.com

ISBN 978-0-8341-4189-6

All rights reserved. No part of this publication may be reproduced, stored in a retrieval system, or transmitted in any form or by any means—for example, electronic, photocopy, recording—without the prior written permission of the publisher. The only exception is brief quotations in printed reviews.

Cover design: Arthur Cherry
Interior design: Sharon Page

Unless otherwise indicated, all Scripture quotations are from the Holy Bible, New International Version® (NIV®). Copyright © 1973, 1978, 1984, 2011 by Biblica, Inc.™ Used by permission of Zondervan. All rights reserved worldwide. www.zondervan.com. The "NIV" and "New International Version" are trademarks registered in the United States Patent and Trademark Office by Biblica, Inc.™

The following version of Scripture is in the public domain:

The King James Version (KJV)

Library of Congress Cataloging-in-Publication Data
A complete catalog record for this book is available from the Library of Congress.

The internet addresses, email addresses, and phone numbers in this book are accurate at the time of publication. They are provided as a resource. The Foundry Publishing® does not endorse them or vouch for their content or permanence.

Contents

1. Frogs and Friends — 7
2. One in Three — 17
3. Creator and Re-creator — 39
4. With or In — 57
5. Immanuel — 75
6. Incarnation — 95
7. Final Instructions — 115
8. Radical Transformation — 135
9. Gifts and Fruit — 157
10. Best Friend Forever — 177

Bibliography — 187

ONE

Frogs and Friends

The L<small>ORD</small> would speak to Moses face to face, as one speaks to a friend.
—Exodus 33:11

He [God] spake not as a prince to a subject, but as a man to his friend, whom he loves, and with whom he takes sweet counsel.
—John Wesley[1]

Classroom Observation

"Give me a word that describes your best friend." Each year for nearly thirty years I began a specific lecture with that request. Students would then volunteer a variety of descriptive words. In my early days of teaching, I wrote each word on a greenboard with a piece of white chalk. As the years passed, whiteboards replaced greenboards, so I wrote each word on the board using a black erasable marker. Finally, whiteboards gave way to Smart Boards, which meant that I entered each word into a computer for display on an interactive whiteboard. Although technology changed from decade to decade, student responses to my request remained amazingly similar from year to year and generation to generation.

Students consistently described their best friends with words such as "hardworking," "loving," "compassionate,"

---

1. John Wesley, *Explanatory Notes upon the Old Testament*, 3 vols. (Bristol, UK: William Pine, 1765; repr., Salem, OH: Schmul, 1975), 1:318-19.

"kind," "funny," "fun loving," "reflective," "appreciative," "caring," "wise," "cheerful," "trusting," "humble," "confident," "thankful," "cooperative," "generous," "courageous," "courteous," "creative," "determined," "helpful," "devoted," "enthusiastic," "fair," "godly," "forgiving," "honest," "independent," "joyful," "kind," "self-disciplined," "loyal," "optimistic," "patient," "reliable," "respectful," "sincere," "thoughtful," and "spiritual." I could go on, but you get the picture!

Every year student responses completely covered the board from one end to the other and from top to bottom. And every year students responded exactly as expected. Look at the list of descriptive words above. Notice an important common characteristic. Do you see it? No student in nearly thirty years of responding to my request ever gave me a physical characteristic to describe his or her best friend. No one ever said, "He has blue eyes," "She has blond hair," "He is short," or "She is tall." Students always named characteristics that identified their best friends' qualities. They would speak of the qualities of a friend's spirit, personality, mindset, or heart. Their responses acknowledged an important feature of personhood—that is, people know us not by how we appear in a mirror or photograph but by who we are as people created in the image of God. Deep down, we all probably intuitively know that, but we do not usually stop to think about it. Keep this thought in mind as we proceed; we will return to it shortly.

A Childhood Pet

Many children around the world ask their parents for a pet at some point in their lives. I grew up on a farm, so my sister, two brothers, and I enjoyed the company of just about every animal common to a family farm. Our pets included dogs, cats, horses, pigs, ducks, geese, rabbits, and chickens. They all had names, and we spent many hours every day giving these animals our undivided attention.

So when our son, Brent, began negotiating with my wife, Sue, and me to get a pet, we were open to his suggestions. The list of options quickly shrank as we took into consideration Sue's allergies to all dogs and cats; our urban residence, which ruled out large barnyard animals; and an open backyard, which ruled out flying fowl. Brent saw a TV ad for an animal show at a local convention center. This show featured one category of pets—reptiles! On the way to the reptile show, Brent and I both had excellent pet options in mind. Unfortunately, they were not the same options. I pictured a cute color-adapting chameleon; Brent was dead set on a snake. We engaged in a long conversation as we walked the aisles of the convention center. He was not in favor of the chameleon, and the snake certainly did not have my vote. Finally, we compromised on an Argentine horned frog. He was a cute little fella, about the size of a small coin, sitting quietly at the bottom of a Styrofoam cup. Brent and I both returned home with a sense of satisfaction: Brent had his new pet, and it was not a snake!

Brent named his new pet Solomon. He cared for Solomon daily as he grew to the size of a man's fist. Solomon's nutrition needs were simple, since he only ate once a week and preferred the same diet at every meal. When he was small, he ate small mice. When he reached adulthood, he feasted on one very large mouse each week. The years passed quickly. Before we knew it, our son graduated from high school and headed off to college. We insisted that he take Solomon with him. One of the highlights of university dorm life occurred when the guys on Brent's hall gathered in his room to watch Solomon enjoy his weekly meal. It happened in a split second, so everyone had to watch carefully. It was remarkably entertaining.

The Holy Spirit is a person and has created us with personhood so we can relate to him, not as a theological concept, but as our best friend.

Keep this entire account also in mind as we continue. We will get back to it very soon.

Lab Exercise

I have one more story to tell before making my point. I attended a high school that required a course in biology. We met for class daily in a science lab. Many decades have passed since I attended that class. I don't suppose I'll ever get the smell of formaldehyde out of my nose. Just thinking about it reminds me of that unpleasant odor. I will also never forget how that smell permeated the air as my lab partner and I fulfilled the course assignment of dissecting a frog. This exercise required carefully opening the underside of a formaldehyde-soaked specimen, exposing all the major organs and body parts, and labeling those organs and body parts with little pushpin flags. I am not sure how that exercise contributed to a better education or fuller life experience for us, but we did it!

A Matter of Perspective

What on earth do friends and frogs have to do with a theological discussion about the Holy Spirit? You may be asking that question by this point, so I will quickly connect the dots. I have read dozens of books devoted solely to presentations on the Holy Spirit. Some have been written in my lifetime; others are hundreds of years old. You may be interested to know that scholars and theologians have been writing books about the Holy Spirit throughout church history. I personally have carried a lingering frustration with most of these books. Why? Because presentations by scholars and theologians tend to identify all the biblical passages in both the Old and New Testaments that speak of God's Spirit. Then they describe all the functions, tasks, or offices of the Spirit. Don't get me wrong; I understand this methodical approach. However, I tend to complete the reading of these books and sense that something essential and significant has been omitted.

Let me illustrate what I am thinking. After I have read a long series of biblical passages that speak of the Holy Spirit or a long series of words that describe his actions, I feel as though I have dissected a subject academically but have missed the intention of Scripture in directing my thoughts toward the third person of the Trinity. In my mind, the Holy Spirit is a person and has created us with personhood so we can relate to him, not as a theological concept, but as our best friend. Solomon and my biology-lab creature were both frogs. My lab frog was nothing more than an object with an educational purpose. Solomon was a pet friend with a name and personality; he was a member of our family. Brent related to Solomon differently than I related to my lab frog.

Too often in Christian music and conversation, we talk about the Holy Spirit as an experience, emotion, or sign. Too many times I have heard musicians sing songs that encourage the congregation to "get *it* on down" in reference to a desire for the Holy Spirit to bless worshippers. Notice the pronoun in that phrase: "it." How would you feel if a friend of yours introduced you to another person and referred to you as it? I think you would feel a bit depersonalized. I wonder if God the Holy Spirit feels something like that when Christians refer to him as a spiritual force, experience, emotion, or sign. Do we want fellowship and an intimate relationship with him? Or do we just want a spiritual buzz for the day?

The purpose of the Bible and theological study goes beyond mastering a body of knowledge. I took a class every semester at a local state university to meet prerequisites for admission into a PhD program. The professor in one of my classes caught me off guard one day. He asked every student in the class to give one reason he or she was taking the class. I said I wanted to use the information to further my studies toward a PhD in the Christian faith. The professor approached me after class and said he envied me for seeking a graduate degree in the Christian faith. I asked him if he was a believer. He indicated that he was not. I then asked why he wished he had a graduate degree in that field of study. He said, "Because people with a PhD degree in the Christian faith are highly respected; I envy the respect they receive." I had never heard that before but have thought a great deal about it across the years.

I think some people study the Bible and theology to master a body of knowledge. I am writing this book, not so you will gather more information about the Holy Spirit, but so you will know him more personally, surrender to him more completely, and be filled with his presence more fully. Please read the pages of this book with that purpose in mind.

Remember the observation from my university classroom exercise. We don't describe a best friend with impersonal, academic traits. We name characteristics that identify qualities of his or her spirit, personality, mindset, or heart. We focus attention on who a best friend is as a person and how we foster a meaningful relationship with that person. That is exactly how I intend to speak about God's Holy Spirit. I trust you will grow in your faith and your relationship with God as we explore a little of the depth of God's self-revelation to us.

But Why?

Most parents go through at least two "But why?" periods while raising their children. The first occurs sometime during the preschool years; the second often happens in the preteen or early teen years. It seems that every parental word of instruction or correction elicits the "But why?" question from children. Some days those questions come at parents like an avalanche. Believers also ask a multitude of "But why?" questions as they learn about the beliefs and practices of the Christian faith. These questions indicate that the believer honestly wants to understand the faith at a deeper level. So throughout this book I have offered numerous biblical references following theological observations. I included these references not just to show that my thoughts have biblical bases but also to give you tools for further study. I want you to read this book with your Bible at your side. Look up the references in your Bible as you read them, mark them for future reference, and read the passages of Scripture before and after the references to understand the context. I pray that the time you spend with this book will give you a deeper love for Scripture and a hunger that will draw you daily to hear the voice of the Holy Spirit speaking through the Word of God.

Words to Describe the Holy Spirit

As you read through this book, you will discover different words describing the Holy Spirit. Some of these words will be listed at the end of each chapter. A final list with all the end-of-chapter words will conclude chapter 10. As you meditate on these words, consider how they amplify your understanding of the Holy Spirit and his work.

1. Almighty
2. Sovereign
3. Creator
4. Friend

Questions for Reflection

1. What misconceptions do your non-Christian friends have about the Holy Spirit?

2. What were some of your misconceptions about the Holy Spirit when you were a new or younger Christian?

3. How has your understanding of the Holy Spirit grown over the years?

4. What are the sources for most of your current beliefs about the Holy Spirit?

5. What do you see as the greatest danger in conceptualizing the Holy Spirit as a "force" rather than as a person?

6. What do you see as the greatest danger in studying the Bible and theology simply to master a body of knowledge?

TWO

One in Three

Therefore go and make disciples of all nations, baptizing them in the name of the Father and of the Son and of the Holy Spirit.
—Matthew 28:19

I know not how any one can be a Christian believer till he "hath," as St. John speaks, "the witness in himself;" till "the Spirit of God witnesses with his spirit, that he is a child of God;" that is, in effect, till God the Holy Ghost witnesses that God the Father has accepted him through the merits of God the Son: And, having this witness, he honours the Son, and the blessed Spirit, "even as he honours the Father."
—John Wesley[1]

Imagine This

One morning you wake up and decide you would like to learn everything you can about a new hobby you want to pursue. After eating breakfast, you warm up the computer and google the hobby. The Google search engine yields one hundred million articles, videos, blogs, and photographs related to your hobby. Realizing you cannot access all one hundred million search results, you attempt to download them onto a flash drive. Your computer works for about ten seconds and then stops and displays the message "Out of Memory."

---

1. John Wesley, "On the Trinity," in *The Works of John Wesley*, 3rd ed., ed. Thomas Jackson, 14 vols. (London: Wesleyan Methodist Book Room; repr., Grand Rapids: Baker Book House, 1979), 6:205.

Clearly your internet search yielded web addresses to more articles, videos, blogs, and photographs than your memory storage device could record. Therein lies our problem. We are divinely created human beings. God gave us a brain that provides us with incredible intellectual processing capacities, reasoning abilities, and a storage bank to retain information that goes beyond even our ability to comprehend. However, our God-given brain does not have an unlimited ability for processing intellectual concepts, reasoning, or storage. It hits its limits quickly.

God our creator is uncreated. In fact, God's existence far exceeds our understanding of "being." He is the source of being. He lives from everlasting to everlasting. There was never a time when he was not. He is unlimited in his capacities and abilities. He can do anything that does not defy his nature. No storage device on earth or in heaven can contain all the information that could be gathered about him. Therefore, it stands to reason that our created brain can never fully comprehend all that can be known about Creator God. To put it another way, if God were to begin an information dump about himself into our brains, they would overload and shut down in a second.

Suprarational

Our brains can only rationally or logically process a limited number of Christian faith statements. That does not mean these faith statements are irrational or illogical. It means that some of the doctrines of our Christian faith go beyond our limited human capacity. One of those doctrines, taught from the early days of Christian history, is the doctrine of the Trinity.

The doctrine of the Trinity states that God is three persons in one being or substance. Granted, we do not find the word "trinity" within the pages of the Bible. However, we read hints of the presence and operation of the Trinity throughout the Old Testament and find a clear view of the Trinity in the New Testament.

Genesis 1:1 introduces God as the creator of everything we know. It also references the Spirit of God hovering over the work of this creation. Although Genesis 1–2 does not specifically reference Jesus Christ, John 1:3 says of Jesus's involvement in creation, "Through him all things were made; without him nothing was made that has been made." The Old Testament says God's Spirit came upon the seventy elders (Num. 11:25), Balaam (24:2), Othniel (Judg. 3:10), Gideon (6:34), Samson (14:6), Saul (1 Sam. 10:10), and David (16:13). David, in his prayer of repentance in Psalm 51, prayed, "Do not cast me from your presence or take your Holy Spirit from me" (v. 11).

The New Testament presents a clearer picture of God as Father, Son, and Spirit. We will explore this idea in greater depth in later chapters. For now, notice the presence of all three members of the Trinity at the baptism of Jesus in Matthew 3:16-17. Recall the Great Commission of Jesus to his disciples in Matthew 28:18-20: "Then Jesus came to them and said, 'All authority in heaven and on earth has been given to me. Therefore go and make disciples of all nations, baptizing them in the name of the Father and of the Son and of the Holy Spirit, and teaching them to obey everything I have commanded you. And surely I am with you always, to the very end of the age.'" Likewise, Paul prayed with a Trinitarian outline: "May the grace of the Lord Jesus Christ, and the love of God, and the fellowship of the Holy Spirit be with you all" (2 Cor. 13:14). Peter agreed when he said, "To God's elect, . . . , who have been chosen according to the foreknowledge of God the Father, through the sanctifying work of the Spirit, to be obedient to Jesus Christ and sprinkled with his blood: Grace and peace be yours in abundance" (1 Pet. 1:1-2).

We often talk about attributes or characteristics of God. All of these attributes or characteristics, and many more that we could never exhaustively list, apply to God the Father, Son, and Holy Spirit.

Historically, early Christian church leaders realized that indications of the Trinity in Jewish and Christian experience resulted in a mathematical, logical, and rational problem that exceeded their ability to solve. They studied, researched, worked, prayed, and preached the gospel message of Jesus Christ from the firm foundation located within Old Testament scriptural and Jewish tradition. At the same time, the teaching and preaching ministry of Jesus added new concepts to their thinking. The writings and letters (which later became the New Testament) that circulated in the early church from its first one hundred years added important ways of analyzing the faith.

Tertullian (ca. AD 155–ca. AD 220) appears to be the first Christian scholar to attempt a Christian presentation on the Trinity. No one knows if he is the first to use the term. His treatise *Against Praxeas* is the earliest writing currently known on this topic. Tertullian used two important words that found their way into later creedal statements. He presented his understanding of Trinity using the words "substance" and "person." Thus he described God as both one in substance and three in persons. He wrote, "This . . . [is] unity in trinity, . . . Father, Son, and Spirit—three . . . but of one nature and of one reality and of one power, because there is one God."[2]

One church says in its articles of faith,
We believe in one eternally existent, infinite God, Sovereign Creator and Sustainer of the universe; that He only is God, holy in nature, attributes, and purpose. The God who is holy love and light is Triune in essential being, revealed as Father, Son, and Holy Spirit.
(Genesis 1; Leviticus 19:2; Deuteronomy 6:4–5; Isaiah 5:16; 6:1–7; 40:18–31; Matthew 3:16–17;

---

2. Tertullian, *Against Praxeas*, trans. A. Souter (New York: Macmillan, 1920), 30.

28:19–20; John 14:6–27; 1 Corinthians 8:6; 2 Corinthians 13:14; Galatians 4:4–6; Ephesians 2:13–18; 1 John 1:5; 4:8)[3]

This statement of faith offers a variety of descriptions of our triune God, as well as Scriptures for further research. We will attempt in the discussions of this book to explore some of them as we expand our understanding of God the Holy Spirit.

Recognizing the Trinity

We will not devote attention in this book to the many conversations, debates, and councils of biblical scholars and religious leaders that resulted in the early church's formal statements confirming the doctrinal understanding of the Trinity. This book is one volume in a series of studies known as The Wesleyan Theology Series. Samuel Powell wrote a volume in this series titled *The Trinity*. The author does an excellent job of exploring our Christian understanding of the Trinity from biblical, theological, and historical perspectives. You will want to consult this book for a richer understanding of everything involved in giving us our present-day understanding of God as Father, Son, and Holy Spirit.

The book you are now reading will devote full attention to the person and work of the third person of the Trinity. We often talk about attributes or characteristics of God. All of these attributes or characteristics, and many more that we could never exhaustively list, apply to God the Father, Son, and Holy Spirit. We would never identify some of these qualities with one member of the Trinity but not another. What we say of one, we say of all. These include the following:

---

3. *Manual, Church of the Nazarene, 2017–2021* (Kansas City: Nazarene Publishing House, 2017), art. 1.

1. *Spiritual.* God is spirit and does not require a physical body to exist as we do. Thus God does not have any space or location limitations. This attribute introduces us to one of the "omnis" of God: God is omnipresent. He occupies all his creation and beyond all the time. We speak in anthropomorphic terms when referring to the "eyes," "arms," or "feet" of God, but we use such terms, not to accurately describe God, but to assist our limited understanding.

    Biblical accounts sometimes speak of God appearing to people as a person or heavenly messenger. We refer to these divine appearances as theophanies. God appeared to people in these biblical accounts for their recognition and understanding, not as a requirement of God's existence. God appeared in this way to Jacob (Gen. 32:22-32), Isaiah (Isa. 6:1), Ezekiel (Ezek. 1:10), and Daniel (Dan. 7:1). The unique exception to this attribute occurred when Jesus Christ, the second person of the Trinity, came to earth in the incarnation and lived with us for thirty-three years (John 1:1-18; Phil. 2:5-8).
2. *Living.* God ever lives. Our understanding of God differs from the understanding of nearly every other religion practiced in the world. Most people worship in a faith system that honors mythical creatures who never lived at all, other than in the imagination of their creators, or who lived on earth but are now dead. Jeremiah 10:10 reminds us that "the Lord is the true God; he is the living God, the eternal King."

    We received life from our parents just as they did. We mark our days with watches and calendars. We have a birth date, and unless the Lord returns in our lifetime, we will have a death date. We require food, water, and shelter to sustain life. God's life has none of these limitations. He had no birth date and will never die. He does not mark time with calendars or watches. And he requires nothing to sustain life.

3. *Holy.* God defines holiness by his nature in many ways. He is separate from all creation. God's uniqueness places him in categories all his own. Exodus 15:11 asks two important questions: "Who among the gods is like you, Lord? Who is like you—majestic in holiness, awesome in glory, working wonders?" Even the places associated with God's presence remain separate from the ordinary locations of life. Moses removed his sandals as he stood on holy ground before the burning bush of God's presence. The tabernacle and temple represented holy places of God's presence. The Israelites even had a special place reserved for God's presence known as the holy of holies. God defines absolute purity and goodness. The angels sang of God in Isaiah's vision: "Holy, holy, holy is the Lord Almighty; the whole earth is full of his glory" (Isa. 6:3). He remains unstained by all that pollutes our sin-soaked world.

4. *Righteous.* God always does the right thing. This does not mean that the laws of nature or morality stand over God to guide his judgment and conduct. It means that the laws of nature and morality flow from his very being. His actions remain consistent with his holy, righteous character. God testified of this in Isaiah 45:21: "There is no God apart from me, a righteous God and a Savior; there is none but me." Again, in Jeremiah 9:24, God says of himself, "'But let the one who boasts

boast about this: that they have the understanding to know me, that I am the Lord, who exercises kindness, justice and righteousness on earth, for in these I delight,' declares the Lord."

5. *Loving.* Nearly everyone who knows anything about the Christian Bible knows John 3:16: "For God so loved the world that he gave his one and only Son, that whoever believes in him shall not perish but have eternal life." God created everything we know in the universe and our world because he loves us. God revealed himself to us because of that love. God the Son lived among us, taught us about the kingdom of heaven, and died on the cross for our sins because he loves us. God the Holy Spirit comes to live with and in us, bringing us his divine presence because he loves us so much.

6. *Wise.* God knows everything there is to know both in our world and in every other corner of his creation that we know nothing about. God has all the facts about every situation and exercises perfect judgment in analyzing these facts. Of this attribute Job said, "It is unthinkable that God would do wrong, that the Almighty would pervert justice" (Job 34:12). Paul summed it up like this: "Oh, the depth of the riches of the wisdom and knowledge of God! How unsearchable his judgments, and his paths beyond tracing out!" (Rom. 11:33). This attribute introduces us to another of the "omnis" of God: God is omniscient.

7. *Powerful.* God has the power to do whatever he wants to do as he remains consistent with his nature. He would never use his power to violate his nature, but nothing is too hard for him. King Jehoshaphat said it well as he "stood up in the assembly of Judah and Jerusalem at the temple

of the Lord in the front of the new courtyard and said: 'Lord, the God of our ancestors, are you not the God who is in heaven? You rule over all the kingdoms of the nations. Power and might are in your hand, and no one can withstand you'" (2 Chron. 20:5-6). This attribute adds another "omni" of God: God is omnipotent.

8. *Truthful.* John 3:33 speaks of the truthfulness of God: "Whoever has accepted it has certified that God is truthful." He always communicates what is correct. He never omits information to deceive us. He never misleads. His speech remains genuine; he always represents things as they truly are. God cannot and will not violate his nature by lying. Hebrews 6:18 says, "God did this so that, by two unchangeable things in which it is impossible for God to lie, we who have fled to take hold of the hope set before us may be greatly encouraged."

9. *Faithful.* Throughout the pages of Scripture, in a variety of cultures and contexts, across thousands of years of recorded history, God proved himself faithful in all he promised he would do (Deut. 7:9; 1 Kings 8:56; Pss. 36:5; 89:1; 1 Cor. 1:9; 1 Pet. 4:19). God made promises to Abraham two thousand years before Christ came into our world. God's promises seemed more extravagant than Abraham could comprehend (Gen. 12:1-3). Yet God fulfilled those promises to Abraham and his descendants throughout the pages of the Old Testament (Acts 7:1-50). Paul said it well: "The one who calls you is faithful, and he will do it" (1 Thess. 5:24).

10. *Persistent.* God proves his persistence in his dealings with humanity from the garden fall to today. He continues to offer us salvation and a personal relationship across the centuries of time. God

Members of the Trinity may work in different ways with us, but all share in bringing God's plan of salvation to us.

persistently forgave and worked with the Israelites through generations of both their faithfulness and unfaithfulness. The book of Judges illustrates this with the continual cycles of the Hebrew people failing God over and over, getting themselves into trouble with neighboring nations, calling on God for deliverance, and returning to their relationship with him. God offered far more grace than anyone deserved to receive (Judg. 2:16-23). Peter thought he exercised generosity in forgiving a person seven times; Jesus called him to a persistent forgiveness of seventy-seven times. By that, Jesus actually meant to forgive others as many times as they needed it (Matt. 18:21-22).

Our limited human understanding can never grasp the greatness and goodness of our God. The best we can hope is that our study will point us in the direction of a better understanding of the mighty God we love and serve.

We often talk about the work of God in our world. This work includes the creation of the world and every living creature in it, especially humanity (Gen. 1–2); covenants with his people (Exod. 34:10); mighty works in our world (Deut. 3:24); wonders beyond human description (1 Chron. 16:9); helping believers in daily life (Ps. 66:8-9); and offering a plan of salvation for all who trust and believe in him (John 3:16-17).

All of the divine work in our world is done by God—the Father, Son, and Holy Spirit. Remember, we would never identify some of these works with one member of the Trinity but not another. What we say of one, we say of all. Members of the Trinity may work in different ways with us, but all share in bringing God's plan of salvation to us.

The Apostles' Creed

We discuss the doctrines of the Christian faith in the long shadow of Christian orthodoxy, which takes us back to the early days of the church. We seek to remain faithful to the theological traditions passed down to us through the ages. With that in mind, we turn our attention to two early creeds that affirm our understanding of the Holy Spirit. The earliest written version of the Apostles' Creed was found in a document called the Interrogatory Creed of Hippolytus, dating back to AD 215. The current form of the creed is found in the writing of Caesarius of Arles, who died in AD 542. We believe the creed came from baptismal catechisms. Hence, new believers would have memorized this creed before being baptized into the Christian faith. Here is a current translation of the Apostles' Creed:

I believe in God, the Father almighty,
> maker of heaven and earth;
> And in Jesus Christ his only Son our Lord;
> who was conceived by the Holy [Spirit],
> born of the Virgin Mary,
> suffered under Pontius Pilate,
> was crucified, dead, and buried.
> He descended into hell.
> The third day he rose again from the dead.
> He ascended into heaven,
> and [sits] on the right hand of God the Father almighty.
> From thence he shall come to judge the [living] and the dead.

I believe in the Holy [Spirit],
> the holy catholic Church,
> the communion of saints,
> the forgiveness of sins,
> the resurrection of the body,

and the life everlasting. Amen.[4]

Notice the creed is Trinitarian. It is built on the three-part outline of Father, Son, and Holy Spirit. Take another look for a hint at what early church leaders believed they needed to clarify the most at that time in Christian history. The creed devotes one statement to the Father, ten statements to Jesus Christ the Son, and one statement to the Holy Spirit. Possibly the emphasis was placed on Jesus Christ because his deity and standing as the second person of the Trinity had sparked debate and disagreement during this period in church history.

Consider the burden the early church leaders carried in explaining the Christian faith in ways that maintained orthodoxy. No one in either the Jewish or Christian traditions questioned the self-revelation of God the Father in the Old Testament. But when people contemplated the life of Jesus Christ the Son, they encountered an immediate problem. Every believer in the Old Testament knew Deuteronomy by heart. A Jewish man even wore a bracelet on his wrist or a small scroll on his forehead with one particular verse printed on it. Deuteronomy 6:4 says, "Hear, O Israel: The LORD our God, the LORD is *one*" (emphasis added).

The Old Testament clearly states that believers must worship one God. That is the very definition of monotheism. So what do we do with Jesus Christ? Is he divine or not? If he is divine, how should Christians acknowledge his divinity without creating two gods? Hence, the Apostles' Creed declared that the life, ministry, death, and resurrection of Jesus Christ were essential to the self-revelation of God to humanity.

Like you and me, the early church leaders were human, and they had only so much time, attention, and reasoning ability within which to operate. They recognized

---

4. *The Book of Common Prayer* (New York: Seabury Press, 1979), 53-54.

the complexity of the self-revelation of God in Jesus Christ. They had to articulate that correctly for future generations of Christians. They knew the numerous references that Jesus made to the Holy Spirit. They knew the significance of the work of the Holy Spirit on the day of Pentecost and in the life of the early church as recorded in the book of Acts. But at the time, they could say little more than, "I believe in the Holy Spirit." More needed to be said about the Holy Spirit, much more. Leaders in the Christian church would address that matter in future discussions.

The Nicene Creed

About three hundred years after Jesus's ascension, the Christian church sat together for its first ecumenical council and crafted a creed of faith at Nicaea in AD 325. Much had happened in the world and in the church. The Christian faith had spread in amazing ways. It also had encountered increased opposition through persecution and false teachers; opponents had tried to twist Christian beliefs into heresy and dethrone Jesus as Lord. They offered other lords in his place.

To counter these opponents, Christian officials worked for many years even after the council at Nicaea to get the language of the creed just right. They came together again in AD 381 at the First Council of Constantinople and added a few words to the creed that we now know as the Nicene Creed. Here is a recent translation:

We believe in one God,
> the Father, the Almighty,
> maker of heaven and earth,
> of all that is, seen and unseen.

We believe in one Lord, Jesus Christ,
> the only Son of God,
> eternally begotten of the Father,
> God from God, Light from Light,

true God from true God,
begotten, not made,
of one Being with the Father.
Through him all things were made.
For us and for our salvation
> he came down from heaven:
by the power of the Holy Spirit
> he became incarnate from the Virgin Mary,
> and was made man.
For our sake he was crucified under Pontius Pilate;
> he suffered death and was buried.
> On the third day he rose again
> > in accordance with the Scriptures;
> he ascended into heaven
> > and is seated at the right hand of the Father.
He will come again in glory to judge the living and the dead,
> and his kingdom will have no end.
We believe in the Holy Spirit, the Lord, the giver of life,
> who proceeds from the Father and the Son.
> With the Father and the Son he is worshiped and glorified.
> He has spoken through the Prophets.
We believe in one holy catholic and apostolic Church.
We acknowledge one baptism for the forgiveness of sins.
We look for the resurrection of the dead,
> and the life of the world to come. Amen.[5]

---

5. Ibid., 358-59.

You notice right away that when comparing the Apostles' Creed with the Nicene Creed, the later one has much more detail. This reminds us of the heresies that arose in the early days of the church that called true doctrine into question. This first ecumenical creed attempted to reaffirm true doctrine by adding definitive words in key places.

Notice too that this creed adds dimension to the church's understanding of the Holy Spirit. Christian officials continue identifying the conception of Jesus Christ with the work of the Holy Spirit as the Apostles' Creed stated. Then they expounded on the church's understanding of the Holy Spirit. They refer to him as "the Lord, the giver of life." They affirm that he proceeded from the Father and the Son, that we are to worship and glorify him just as we do the Father and the Son, and that he spoke through the Old Testament Prophets of his existence and ministry especially in the church age.

A Common Misunderstanding

A common misunderstanding that found a place in the Christian church has hindered a biblical understanding of the Trinity. Many believers and nonbelievers adopt a negative view of God the Father from certain Old Testament passages of Scripture. They see him as a bloodthirsty tyrant who rules the world with an iron fist and instructs his followers to destroy whole nations of people who do not please him. Take for example Deuteronomy 20:16-18:

> However, in the cities of the nations the Lord your God is giving you as an inheritance, do not leave alive anything that breathes. Completely destroy them—the Hittites, Amorites, Canaanites, Perizzites, Hivites and Jebusites—as the Lord your God has commanded you. Otherwise, they will teach you to follow all the detestable things they do in worshiping their gods, and you will sin against the Lord your God.

How ironic that the same modern-day critics who fault the God of the Old Testament for dealing with godless and sinful nations also fault God for not doing enough to enforce biblical justice in the world. The prophet Habakkuk captured the thought well:

How long, Lord, must I call for help,
> but you do not listen?
Or cry out to you, "Violence!"
> but you do not save?
Why do you make me look at injustice?
> Why do you tolerate wrongdoing?
Destruction and violence are before me;
> there is strife, and conflict abounds.
Therefore the law is paralyzed,
> and justice never prevails.
The wicked hem in the righteous,
> so that justice is perverted. (Hab. 1:2-4)

God's purpose in dealing decisively with entire nations of people always focused on their need to repent of their sins and wicked ways and worship the one, true, and living God (Jer. 18:5-11). God never delighted in dealing with sinfulness, but his holy, righteous, and just nature would not allow him to wink at the damage and destructiveness that sin inflicted on the innocent. Nevertheless, critics to this day reject the God of the Old Testament as a bloodthirsty tyrant.

Likewise, many throughout church history express negative feelings and fear of the Holy Spirit. Some blame this on ancient translations that use the designation "Holy Ghost." The word "ghost" conjures images of disembodied spirits who roam the earth placing curses on unsuspecting people, possessing them, haunting buildings, and causing all manner of natural disasters in our world. Hollywood movies and television shows depicting the bad things ghosts can bring into our world have left little to the imagination. Those

We must see the person and work of God as three in one and one in three.

negative images and beliefs have hindered a biblical understanding of the person and work of the Holy Spirit.

Hence, many who criticize the persons of God the Father and God the Holy Spirit place all of their approval and devotion on God the Son. They love what they read in the four gospels of the New Testament. They call attention to the way Jesus embraced children, empowered women, called for biblical justice, and preached a message of love. That is the God they can serve and proclaim to the world.

Considered together, these three common and popular characterizations of Father, Holy Spirit, and Son ignore a biblical understanding of the Trinity. We are not speaking of three different individuals who work in our world in radically different ways. We are speaking of three persons in one substance. So the lowly and loving Jesus of the incarnation is a picture of the Father and the Holy Spirit. Therefore, we must see the person and work of God as three in one and one in three.

Understanding the Trinity

One of the courses I took in seminary was a one-on-one directed study with one of my professors on the doctrine of the Trinity. The professor assigned me weekly readings, which I would discuss with him when we met. During our last meeting, the professor asked me if the course had met my expectations. I told him that I took the class hoping to gain a better understanding of the Trinity but that I still had more questions than when we started. My professor smiled and said, "Great. That means you understand it!" His comment reminded me that our human minds will never fully grasp the depths of all that can be known about our great God. But we gain great satisfaction in learning more about him every day.

Words to Describe the Holy Spirit

1. Trinity
2. Omnipresent
3. Living
4. Holy
5. Righteous
6. Loving
7. Omniscient
8. Omnipotent
9. Truthful
10. Faithful
11. Persistent

Questions for Reflection

1. Do you find it easy or difficult to accept the Christian doctrines about God that are suprarational?

2. What might make it difficult for non-Christians to accept Christian doctrines about God that are suprarational?

3. What analogies or metaphors have you heard to explain God as Trinity?

4. Which qualities of God discussed in this chapter bring you the greatest strength and help as a believer?

5. Which qualities of God discussed in this chapter do you have the hardest time processing?

6. What does God's love for us teach us about the kind of love he would like us to have for him and one another?

7. What examples of God's persistence have you seen in your life?

8. Why should we read and carefully understand the early creeds of the Christian church?

9. What misconceptions have you heard about the God of the Old Testament?

10. How does a proper understanding of Jesus the Son help us more clearly to understand God the Father and God the Holy Spirit?

THREE

Creator and Re-creator

And the Spirit of God was hovering over the waters.
— Genesis 1:2

The Spirit of God was the first Mover.
— John Wesley[1]

The Holy Spirit in Creation

Recent developments in human DNA research have led to a wide variety of applications in daily life. Police detectives can now solve cold-case crimes with DNA analysis. Individuals convicted of crimes they did not commit are being released regularly after having spent decades in a penitentiary. Practically anyone today can purchase a DNA kit, submit a sample, and receive a report on family ancestors traced back for many generations.

Imagine that you purchased a DNA kit, submitted a sample, and were amazed at the report you received about your ancestors. Rather than going back a few generations, your report extended back to the day of creation. If such a report were possible, you would learn about the Holy Spirit's direct involvement in what would become your life. Remember from the last chapter that all three members of the Trinity are involved when we read scriptural accounts

---

1. Wesley, *Explanatory Notes upon the Old Testament*, 1:3 (comment on Gen. 1:2).

about the work of God in our world. Some people mistakenly think that God the Father performed all the divine work of the Old Testament, God the Son came to earth and did the work of God recorded in the first four books of the New Testament, and God the Holy Spirit got involved in the salvation plan for humanity on the day of Pentecost and continues to work with humanity in the church age right up to today. This sounds simple enough but does not prove true when examined in the light of Scripture. A careful examination of Genesis 1–2 indicates that the Holy Spirit worked in significant ways to bring our world and everything in it to reality. Let's explore this passage of Scripture to see how God's Spirit participated in creation.

No news crews stood on the scene with reporters and video cameras rolling on creation day. So we will imagine what the message of Genesis 1 might have looked like. What would a videographer have recorded in the moments before God spoke creation into existence *ex nihilo*?[2] Nothing. God did not begin creation with preexistent matter. He first spoke that matter into existence (v. 1). The next verse of Scripture introduces us to the Holy Spirit: "The Spirit of God was hovering over the waters." The Bible describes matter as "formless," "empty," dark, and chaotic.

The work of God's Spirit "hovering over" can also be translated as "brooding over." John Wesley pointed out the parental watch-care implied in that translation.

> The Spirit of God was the first Mover; He moved upon the face of the waters - He moved upon the face of the deep, as the hen gathereth her chicken[s] under her wings, and hovers over them, to warm and cherish them [Matt. 23:37], as the eagle stirs up her nest, and

---

2. The English translation is "out of nothing."

There is no way of going back to a moment when the Trinity did not exist.

fluttereth over her young ('tis the same word that is here used) [Deut. 32:11].[3]

Notice the parental watch-care of the mother hen gathering her chicks under her wings to lovingly protect them. Notice also the mother eagle caring for the nest of her young eaglets as she flutters over them. The Holy Spirit did not hover over the dark, deep water like a disinterested observer. Rather, the Holy Spirit moved over the water as a parent lovingly preparing a worthy home for all the birds of the air, creatures of the sea, animals of the earth, and especially humanity. He perhaps had millions of ideas about how to make this the perfect place for all that he would bring to life.

Before we look further at the creation account and the role of the Holy Spirit in it, let's go back eight hours prior to the moment of creation. Now we have a problem; our clocks do not work because God the Father, Son, and Holy Spirit existed together eternally before time as we know it. There is no way of going back to a moment when the Trinity did not exist. Our triune God "exists" from eternity past to eternity future.

Theologians sometimes observe that we should not even use the word "exist" in reference to God, since it calls attention to the reality of a being. God is greater than our understanding of being; he is uncreated. God acknowledged that in his conversation with Moses at the burning bush. "Moses said to God, 'Suppose I go to the Israelites and say to them, "The God of your fathers has sent me to you," and they ask me, "What is his name?" Then what shall I tell them?' God said to Moses, 'I AM WHO I AM. This is what you are to say to the Israelites: "I AM has sent me to

---

3. Wesley, *Explanatory Notes upon the Old Testament*, 1:3 (comment on Gen. 1:2).

you"'" (Exod. 3:13-14). God is beyond the categories of being and is the very source of all being. His name is "I am."

With our imagination we see the breath of the Holy Spirit moving over created matter as the "first Mover" of creation, bringing order and definition from chaos. Job described it by saying, "By his breath the skies became fair" (Job 26:13). We see that the Holy Spirit was directly involved in creating the world in which our ancestors lived. Genesis 1:3-25 narrates the divine creation of everything in each succeeding day. The orderly and rhythmic way God speaks the world and everything else into existence suggests a question. Why did God create across periods of time rather than all in one moment?

John Wesley suggested that "the Creator could have made his work perfect at first, but by this gradual proceeding he would [show] what is ordinarily the method of his providence and grace."[4] That spiritual insight addresses an age-old question people have asked throughout human history—namely, "Why does God not answer my prayers on my timetable?" Many of us fall into the temptation of questioning God's timing for helping us with the difficult circumstances of life. Genesis 1 reminds us that God's providence and grace are always at work in the created order and in our lives, even when we do not see the evidence of it. We must choose either to lose faith in him because he does not submit to our planned schedule or to build up faith in him and trust his timing—even when it is difficult for us to see how he will meet our needs.

Genesis 1:3-25 offers little more than a thumbnail sketch of God's creation of the vast expanse of the universe from the far reaches of space to the depths of earth's seas, from the eastern horizon to the western skies of the earth. Then God created living beings to dwell on the earth, in the

---

4. Ibid.

sky, and under the waters of the sea. The narrative changes in verse 26 as Scripture details the crowning moment of God's incredible creating activity: "Then God said, 'Let us make mankind in our image, in our likeness, so that they may rule over the fish in the sea and the birds in the sky, over the livestock and all the wild animals, and over all the creatures that move along the ground.' So God created mankind in his own image, in the image of God he created them; male and female he created them" (vv. 26-27).

Genesis 2 offers more detail concerning the creation of humanity. Here we see the Holy Spirit not just hovering over raw matter as we saw earlier but personally bending down and blowing the breath of life into the nostrils of the human being he had molded from the dust of the earth. "Then the LORD God formed a man from the dust of the ground and breathed into his nostrils the breath of life, and the man became a living being" (v. 7). Again, Job described it by saying, "As long as I have life within me, the breath of God in my nostrils . . ." (Job 27:3). God's breath of life has been passed from parents to children through each generation from the day of humanity's creation until the breath each of us now takes. The Holy Spirit has thus played an important role in all our lives from our very first breaths![5]

We must never take for granted the breath the Holy Spirit carefully blew in Adam's nostrils. Most people in our world like to believe they are self-sufficient; they often refer to themselves as self-made individuals. Science and technology try to convince us that they have, or can quickly find, all the answers to all the needs of our lives. Neither assumption is true. The average person takes between seventeen thousand and twenty-three thousand breaths per day. Every single breath we breathe each day comes to us

---

5. Joseph Coleson, *Genesis 1-11*, New Beacon Bible Commentary (Kansas City: Beacon Hill Press of Kansas City, 2012), 65-69.

as a gift from the Holy Spirit. Science and technology have indeed amazed us with many discoveries and inventions to make life more enjoyable. However, they have never produced a living, breathing person, and they will never do so. God alone authors human life. We must never take that precious gift of life for granted. The psalmist spoke of this when he said of all living creatures on the earth, "When you take away their breath, they die and return to the dust. When you send your Spirit, they are created, and you renew the face of the ground" (Ps. 104:29-30).

Our review of Genesis 1–2 introduces us to the work of the Holy Spirit in several ways. First, his appearance on the scene before the first day of creation tells us, as mentioned above, that he exists before time, before the created matter of our universe, and before the laws of nature that give order and design to all that functions so precisely in our universe. Second, we see him act, not as an impersonal force of nature, but as a person with the intelligence and imagination to envision our wonderful world. Third, he has the power and ability to bring things imagined into reality. It is one thing to spin a big dream; it is quite another to bring that big dream to life.

The Holy Spirit in Providence

The biblical account of God's creative work in Genesis 1 ends with these words, "By the seventh day God had finished the work he had been doing; so on the seventh day he rested from all his work. Then God blessed the seventh day and made it holy, because on it he rested from all the work of creating that he had done" (2:2-3). After reading those words you may ask what God did next in his creation. Some think that when God completed the creative work outlined in Genesis 1–2, he sat back on his heavenly throne, looked

God's Spirit is very likely as involved in holding back the chaos of our world and keeping order in creation as he originally did in the beginning.

out a heavenly panoramic window, and watched all that he created function as he intended it.[6]

That view does not accurately reflect the hundreds of examples in Scripture where we see God intervening in human history and involving himself in our daily lives. From evening walks in the garden of Eden with Adam and Eve (Gen. 3:8) to the incarnation of Jesus Christ (John 1:14), God the Father, Son, and Holy Spirit has been actively working in our world and with us for as long as creation has existed. Psalm 104 praises God for his magnificent works not only in creating the world but also in preserving it from day to day, season to season, and year to year. The verbs throughout this psalm are in the present tense—that is, occurring not in the past, on creation day, but now. The psalmist said God "makes springs" (v. 10), "give[s] water" (v. 11), and "makes grass grow" (v. 14). Every living creature depends on the daily providence of God: "All creatures look to you to give them their food at the proper time" (v. 27).

Paul offered an important insight into this subject when he spoke of Christ Jesus: "For in him all things were created: things in heaven and on earth, visible and invisible, whether thrones or powers or rulers or authorities; all things have been created through him and for him. He is before all things, and in him all things *hold together*" (Col. 1:16-17; emphasis added).

Remember in the previous chapter of this book we affirmed that we believe God is the Trinity and that the persons of the Trinity work together in all that God does. Colossians 1:17 highlights the sustaining providential work of Jesus Christ in holding all things in creation together. "As the agent of creation, he is also the one who gives coher-

---

6. Deism teaches this view. See G. C. Joyce, "Deism," in vol. 4 of *Encyclopedia of Religion and Ethics*, ed. James Hastings (New York: Scribner, 1955), 5-11.

ence to all its parts. Were this not so, *chaos* would overtake an orderly *cosmos* causing its disintegration."⁷

This sustaining work of Jesus is like home maintenance. Any homeowner will tell you that keeping everything in a home maintained and in good working order can be a full-time job. We use the phrase "deferred maintenance" when a homeowner gets behind his or her regular duties and let's things slip into disrepair. Paul affirms that Jesus Christ does not practice deferred maintenance; Jesus maintains the order of all creation all the time. We seldom stop to think about how dependent we are on God's providential sustenance of all we see and know in our world.

Consider this question: Since the Holy Spirit hovered over the chaos during the creative process, could he still, to this day, be providentially hovering over the created order in tandem with the Father and Son? Although a definitive answer is not forthcoming, God's Spirit is very likely as involved in holding back the chaos of our world and keeping order in creation as he originally did in the beginning. Charles Webb Carter said about this question, "Though *implicit* in the Old Testament, rather than *explicit* as in the New Testament, the Holy Spirit is essential to an understanding of the Old Testament record. To neglect or omit the person and function of the Holy Spirit from any serious study of the Old Testament is to render it meaningless."⁸

The Holy Spirit in Re-creation

I have spent countless hours, first with our son and now with our grandchildren, building LEGO toys. Anyone familiar with this activity knows it involves hundreds

---

7. George Lyons, Robert W. Smith, and Kara Lyons-Pardue, *Ephesians, Colossians, Philemon,* New Beacon Bible Commentary (Kansas City: Beacon Hill Press of Kansas City, 2019), 290.

8. Charles Webb Carter, *The Person and Ministry of the Holy Spirit: A Wesleyan Perspective* (Grand Rapids: Baker, 1974), 40.

or thousands of colored plastic blocks and shapes and an instruction manual with detailed directions for proper assembly. This activity requires a keen eye for locating the exact pieces needed to complete each step, fine motor skills to insert delicate pieces into tight spots, and more patience than I can adequately describe!

The next topic for consideration concerning the Holy Spirit's work reminds me of a recent LEGO project my grandson Micah and I completed. We built a remote-controlled car that responded to commands from a computer-tablet app. After many hours of tedious labor building the car, I gave Micah the tablet with the control app so he could test-drive our new creation. He had the car going forward, backward, and in all sorts of patterns in no time. Shortly after I left the room, Micah came to me with tears in his eyes and hands filled with random LEGO pieces. His car had just had an accident! He looked at me with sad, puppy-dog eyes: "Poppy, you helped me build it. Now, can you fix it?" I told him I could and then spent the next half hour patiently putting the car back together.

We started this chapter with the Holy Spirit hovering over chaos and disorder prior to creation. Now we will turn to the work of the Holy Spirit following the fall (Gen. 3). Adam and Eve's disobedience brought not only expulsion from the garden but also a rupture in their relationship with God and damage to the moral image with which God created them. Until the time of their disobedience, the moral image of Adam and Eve was pure, but untested. Once the serpent planted doubt in their minds and suggested that they yield to temptation, they found themselves in the midst of a moral test that they failed. From Genesis 3 through the rest of the Old Testament and from Matthew to Revelation in the New Testament, we find the Holy Spirit actively involved in restoring humanity to the way God created humans to be.

We Need a Messiah

The work of the Holy Spirit in empowering individuals in the Old Testament to accomplish certain tasks was an important part of fulfilling God's will for the Israelites. We will discuss several of these individuals and the work the Spirit gave them in the next chapter. Of greater importance, however, was the work of the Holy Spirit in God's redemptive plan for the salvation of humanity. We needed the forgiveness of our sins, a restored relationship with our heavenly Father, and a reclaimed identity as children of God. In short, we needed a Messiah.

Much of the Holy Spirit's work in the Old Testament focused on preparing the way for the coming Messiah. This is an important interpretive key to understanding the overarching message of the entire Old Testament. We would never find our way back to God by our own initiative or effort. If we were to receive forgiveness, restoration, and a new identity with God, he would have to offer the plan of salvation to us and assist us in responding to his offer. To that end the Holy Spirit worked, often quietly across the centuries, until as Paul put it, "But *when the set time had fully come*, God sent his Son, born of a woman, born under the law" (Gal. 4:4; emphasis added). If you have ever planned an important social event for a large number of people, you know the thousands of detail that go into those plans and the importance of everything coming together at the appointed time for the event. Preparation for the coming of our Savior Jesus Christ was no different. The Holy Spirit worked to have every detail in place for the Messiah's coming at the "set time."

Just as the Holy Spirit brooded over the dark chaotic waters to bring order to the chaos, he also brooded over the chaos in the hearts of humanity darkened by sin and alienated from relationship with their creator. The Holy Spirit breathed the breath of life into Adam's nostrils, and he became a living soul. Likewise, the Spirit worked to draw lost souls back to the heart of their creator so he could breathe spiritual life into them. The Holy Spirit worked diligently in this re-creative work throughout the Old Testament to restore what was lost in the fall. That period of salvation history looked forward to the coming of the Messiah. We have the privilege of living in the church age, so we look back to the Messiah's first coming. From the time Adam and Eve left the garden of Eden until the end of time as we know it, the Holy Spirit has been and will be at work completing the divine redemptive plan.

The Spirit would love nothing more than to have everyone experience what Paul described in 2 Corinthians 5:17: "Therefore, if anyone is in Christ, the new creation has come: The old has gone, the new is here!" The King James Version translates it like this: "Therefore if any man be in Christ, he is a new creature: old things are passed away; behold, all things are become new." Both translations call our attention to the reality that God's plan of salvation makes us new creatures in Christ living in God's new spiritual creation until the end of time and the eternal restoration of all things. "He who was seated on the throne said, 'I am making everything new!'" (Rev. 21:5). Peter spoke of that day as he preached at Solomon's Colonnade following the healing of the lame beggar: "Heaven must receive him [Jesus] until the time comes for God to restore everything, as he promised long ago through his holy prophets" (Acts 3:21).

Genesis 1:27 introduces a profound idea about our created identity that we have not yet explored. It says, "So God created mankind in his own image, in the image of God he created them." Entire books explore the ways in which God created humanity in his own image. We do not have time to explore all of those ways. However, we need to examine a couple of them that relate to the work of the Holy Spirit in our re-creation.

First, God created us with a moral image—that is, we have an internal moral compass that alerts us to right and wrong as we make daily choices. Our conscience represents one example of the way that moral compass functions within us. When we heed our conscience and continue to make right choices, the accuracy of our conscience remains true and guides us in paths of righteousness. However, if we ignore the alerts and warnings of our conscience, we dull our sensitivity to it. Our mind and heart grow dark, and we lose our way morally. Paul addressed this matter in Romans 1:18-32. He painted a heartbreaking picture of the end result of those who rebel against their God-given moral compass. He concluded this passage by saying, "Although they know God's righteous decree that those who do such things deserve death, they not only continue to do these very things but also approve of those who practice them" (v. 32). When we turn in faith to Christ, the Holy Spirit works within us to re-create us in the moral image of God. This empowers us to live lives of righteousness and holiness (Heb. 12:22-24).

Second, the image of God in us makes possible a relationship with our creator. For me, the beauty of nature, the abundance of food, and the comfort of a perfect environment were not the most inviting features of the garden of Eden. They provided a wonderful home, but they were not what truly made the garden a paradise. My heart is drawn to the evening walks and conversations the first couple enjoyed with their creator. My mind cannot even begin to process the utter ecstasy of that unhindered relationship. That is why the re-creative work of the Holy Spirit seeks to restore a vital, personal relationship with our creator. He wants to be in constant fellowship with us.

King David ruled Israel in an era known as the golden age of his people. He ruled well and made many wise decisions as the spiritual and civil leader. He also left us a

The Holy Spirit guided the development of Scripture at every juncture and inspires the Word of God as we read it.

wonderful collection of psalms to use in the worship and praise of God. But Psalm 51 recounts one of the dark events of David's life; he sinned against Uriah and committed adultery with Bathsheba. Hear the cry of his heart as he confessed his sins before God and sought a restoration of their relationship: "Hide your face from my sins and blot out all my iniquity. Create in me a pure heart, O God, and renew a steadfast spirit within me. Do not cast me from your presence or take your Holy Spirit from me" (vv. 9-11). David rightly understood that only the work of the Holy Spirit could restore the relationship God wanted to have with him.

Earlier we spoke of the Holy Spirit working, often quietly behind the scenes, during the Old Testament period. What was he doing in preparation for the coming Messiah? Many things. For example, he spoke through God's prophets about things to come in God's salvation history. We reference many of these prophecies in this book. Then he inspired the authors of the books in the Old Testament to accurately record the prophets' messages. He also preserved these writing across many generations through numerous persecutions and attempts to destroy them. Furthermore, he worked with translators and translation committees to translate the prophets' messages into multiple languages. Finally, the Spirit opens our eyes and ears in faith as we read these messages so that we hear God's Word deep within our hearts and minds. Each of these works of the Spirit contributed to what we know as the inspiration of Scripture. The Holy Spirit guided the development of Scripture at every juncture and inspires the Word of God as we read it.

Four times in Genesis 1 God reached the end of a creation day, looked over his handiwork, and concluded that "it was good" (vv. 10, 12, 18, 21). At the end of the sixth day, he made a panoramic review of all he had created and concluded that "it was very good" (v. 31). God has all wisdom and knowledge and has perfect judgment to assess every situation correctly. So we can take God's word for it that everything he created was very good. The Holy Spirit's re-creation work seeks to restore the hearts and lives of every disciple of Christ to wholeness, completeness, and a relationship with God that is deeply personal as he or she journeys together with other believers until all reach their final heavenly home.

Words to Describe the Holy Spirit

1. Eternal
2. Re-creator
3. Sustainer

Questions for Reflection

1. How do you visualize the nothingness that "existed" before God spoke our world into existence?

2. What emotions and feelings might the Holy Spirit have had as he brooded over the chaos of raw elements before bringing us into the world?

3. How do you process the reality that God the Father, Son, and Holy Spirit exist from eternity past to eternity future?

4. How has the providence of God been at work in your life?

5. How do you visualize what would happen to us and our world if God ever removed his providential hand?

6. How does the Holy Spirit's work of re-creation in our lives compare to his original creative work?

7. Why do you think God the Holy Spirit takes such concerned care of you?

8. How do you process the notion that you are created in the image of God?

9. Why was a Messiah so necessary for our spiritual lives?

10. Why did the Holy Spirit give so many clues about the coming Messiah over such a long period of time?

FOUR

With or In

But you know him [the Spirit of Truth], for he lives with you and will be in you.

—John 14:17

That we "must be baptized with the Holy Ghost," implies this and no more, that we cannot be "renewed in righteousness and true holiness" any otherwise than by being over-shadowed, quickened, and animated by that blessed Spirit.

—John Wesley[1]

A Love Story

My wife and I met on a Christian university campus. She was in her second year of college; I was a senior. We went to church together on our first date. We enjoyed each other's company, so we began attending worship services together every week. We soon added study dates in the campus library. That probably was not a good idea, since I found myself looking up from the book I was reading just to stare at her. She would catch me staring, and I would have to return to my reading. We also traveled every other weekend with a group of university students to churches within driving distance to sing and preach. We got to know each other pretty well over the next year and a half. During

---

1. Wesley, "An Extract of a Letter to the Reverend Mr. Law," in *Works of John Wesley*, 9:495.

that time our relationship grew from casual dating to going steady, to engagement, and then to marriage.

We pledged our love for each other several decades ago. Our relationship has grown and developed over the years. In the first eighteen months of our dating relationship, we spent time together sitting, talking, worshipping, studying, laughing, and crying. We were with each other in a variety of locations and activities. After we married, our relationship shifted to an entirely different level. We shared life together as husband and wife and soon knew each other's habits, routines, and moods and sometimes each other's thoughts. We began to finish each other's sentences. We could read each other's facial expressions or body language. Our love for each other gives us a connection that brings us together in the mysterious way that Jesus described when he said, "'For this reason a man will leave his father and mother and be united to his wife, and the two will become one flesh.' . . . So they are no longer two, but one flesh. Therefore what God has joined together, let no one separate" (Matt. 19:5-6).

This simple illustration does not perfectly illustrate the transition that takes place between the Old and New Testaments in the way the Holy Spirit interacts with believers. However, it offers a brief glimpse at the miraculous progression in God's self-revelation to humanity from God's Spirit being *with* believers to his Spirit being *in* them. Let's look at the way the Bible describes it.

Examples of God's Spirit *with* Believers in the Old Testament

Strong's Exhaustive Concordance of the Bible names about one hundred references to the Spirit of God in the Old Testament. About three-fourths of them refer to the Holy Spirit working with individuals externally.[2] In other words, he was *with* people in unique ways. Here are a few examples.

God's Spirit gave Bezalel and Oholiab the supernatural ability to understand and execute God's plan for the construction of the tabernacle.

> Then the Lord said to Moses, "See, I have chosen Bezalel son of Uri, the son of Hur, of the tribe of Judah, and I have filled him with the Spirit of God, with wisdom, with understanding, with knowledge and with all kinds of skills—to make artistic designs for work in gold, silver and bronze, to cut and set stones, to work in wood, and to engage in all kinds of crafts. Moreover, I have appointed Oholiab son of Ahisamak, of the tribe of Dan, to help him. Also I have given ability to all the skilled workers to make everything I have commanded you: the tent of meeting, the ark of the covenant law with the atonement cover on it, and all the other furnishings of the tent—the table and its articles, the pure gold lampstand and all its accessories, the altar of incense, the altar of burnt offering and all its utensils, the basin with its stand—and also the woven garments, both the sacred garments for Aaron the priest and the garments for his sons when they serve as priests, and the anointing oil and fragrant incense for the Holy Place. They are to make them just as I commanded you." (Exod. 31:1-11)

Notice the detail and specificity with which God gifted these two men so they could comprehend the grand vision of God for a worship center for the Hebrew people. Not only did the Spirit help them understand God's plan, but also God's Spirit gave them the supernatural skill and craftsmanship to bring the grand vision to reality right down to the smallest detail.

---

2. Carter, *Person and Ministry*, 60.

The Spirit of the Lord gave several Old Testament prophets the ability to see ahead to a new chapter in God's plan for our salvation. They saw a day when the Holy Spirit would not just be *with* believers; he would abide *in* them.

A common phrase occurs often in the historical books of the Old Testament: "The Spirit of the Lord came upon . . ." God empowered Othniel, as recorded in Judges 3:10: "The Spirit of the Lord came on him, so that he became Israel's judge and went to war. The Lord gave Cushan-Rishathaim king of Aram into the hands of Othniel, who overpowered him." God worked in a similar way in the life of Gideon: "Then the Spirit of the Lord came on Gideon, and he blew a trumpet, summoning the Abiezrites to follow him" (6:34). The Bible says of Samson, "The Spirit of the Lord came powerfully upon him so that he tore the lion apart with his bare hands as he might have torn a young goat" (14:6). King Saul received the ability to prophesy from God's Spirit: "When he and his servant arrived at Gibeah, a procession of prophets met him; the Spirit of God came powerfully upon him, and he joined in their prophesying" (1 Sam. 10:10). God's Spirit came upon David as the prophet Samuel anointed him the next king of Israel: "So Samuel took the horn of oil and anointed him in the presence of his brothers, and from that day on the Spirit of the Lord came powerfully upon David" (16:13).

God's Spirit worked *with* each of these Old Testament personalities, from Bezalel to David, along with many others. The Holy Spirit gave them a supernatural ability to fulfill the work God gave them to do. The Spirit of God came upon them for a season to accomplish his divine will. As wonderful as this endowment with divine ability was in those days, the Spirit of the Lord gave several Old Testament prophets the ability to see ahead to a new chapter in God's plan for our salvation. They saw a day when the Holy Spirit would not just be *with* believers; he would abide *in* them. Listen to a few of these proclamations of things to come.

"The days are coming," declares the Lord,
    "when I will make a new covenant
  with the people of Israel

>   and with the people of Judah.
> It will not be like the covenant
>   I made with their ancestors
> when I took them by the hand
>   to lead them out of Egypt,
> because they broke my covenant,
>   though I was a husband to them,"
>   declares the Lord.
> "This is the covenant I will make with the people of
>   Israel
>   after that time," declares the Lord.
> "I will put my law in their minds
>   and write it on their hearts.
> I will be their God,
>   and they will be my people." (Jer. 31:31-33)

Jeremiah ministered in a day when the Hebrew people knew nothing but discouragement and defeat. They experienced firsthand the invasion of enemy nations that forced them to trade their homes, their possessions, and their familiar routines for captivity in a foreign land. Jeremiah spoke not only about God remaining faithful to them through this horrible exile but also about the hope that God would return them to their homeland and someday enter into a new covenant relationship with them.

The use of the phrase "new covenant" in verse 31 quickly catches our attention because it is the only verse in the Old Testament that tells the people of that generation that a new covenant between God and humanity would be coming. The Israelites at that time knew only of the covenants God made with Noah, Abraham, and Moses on Mount Sinai, which resulted in the Ten Commandments. Jeremiah received a glimpse into the future when God would do a "new thing" (31:22) in revealing a deeper understanding of himself. The new thing would open the way for believers to have a deeper relationship with God through the infilling of the Holy Spirit. This new covenant would not be an upgraded version of an old one but an entirely new one.[3]

This language does not sound unusual to those of us living in the twenty-first century. We reference it often when we call the last twenty-seven books in the Bible the New Testament. This New Testament tells us everything we need to know about God's new covenant with humanity, about a new way of salvation through Jesus Christ, and about a deeper relationship with God.[4]

We know Jeremiah spoke of a deeper relationship with God when he used the imagery of one of the most sacred of all relationships known to humanity—the relationship between husband and wife. God said that Israel's unfaithfulness to their covenantal relationship with him resulted in a ruptured relationship. Jeremiah 2 and 3 spoke of that rupture. Hosea 2 and 3 also referenced it. Though Israel, the wife in this imagery, became unfaithful, God remained faithful as a loving and loyal husband to her. Rather than giving up on the relationship, God promised a day when he would enter into a brand-new covenant with his children.[5]

Jeremiah 31:33 does not refer to a new set of commandments or rules being implanted in the minds and hearts of believers. Rather, it refers to a new presence of God living in minds and hearts that fosters a new type of divine love toward God, others, and oneself. The clouded mystery of this prophecy in Jeremiah's day broke into the bright sunlight of God's self-revelation on the day of Pentecost, when Jesus's disciples received the infilling of the Holy Spirit, the third person of the Trinity! To this day, we live

---

3. Alex Varughese and Mitchel Modine, *Jeremiah 26–52*, New Beacon Bible Commentary (Kansas City: Beacon Hill Press of Kansas City, 2010), 151-52.
4. Other references to the new covenant by Jeremiah appear in 24:7; 32:37-40; 50:5. See also Malachi 3:1.
5. Varughese and Modine, *Jeremiah 26–52*, 152-53.

in the bright sunlight of the Spirit's presence in our minds and hearts, transforming us into the image of Jesus Christ (Rom. 8:29).[6]

Paul recognized the fulfillment of Jeremiah's prophecy in the lives of Christian believers: "You show that you are a letter from Christ, the result of our ministry, written not with ink but with the Spirit of the living God, not on tablets of stone but on tablets of human hearts" (2 Cor. 3:3). Likewise, the writer of the book of Hebrews quoted Jeremiah and saw the prophecy's fulfillment in the life of the early Christian church (Heb. 8:10; 10:16). Hence, New Testament writers agree that God gave Jeremiah a vision of the coming incarnation of God in Christ Jesus.

God spoke through the prophet Ezekiel with this incredible promise:

> I will sprinkle clean water on you, and you will be clean; I will cleanse you from all your impurities and from all your idols. I will give you a new heart and put a new spirit in you; I will remove from you your heart of stone and give you a heart of flesh. And I will put my Spirit in you and move you to follow my decrees and be careful to keep my laws. Then you will live in the land I gave your ancestors; you will be my people, and I will be your God. (Ezek. 36:25-28)

The context of this passage begins in verse 22, where God instructed Ezekiel to say, "Therefore say to the Israelites, 'This is what the Sovereign Lord says: It is not for your sake, people of Israel, that I am going to do these things, but for the sake of my holy name, which you have profaned among the nations where you have gone.'" The Bible often uses the word "therefore" as a transition or hinge word signaling a change in thought. Ezekiel reviewed the unfaithfulness of God's people while living in the promised land

---

6. Ibid., 153-55.

(vv. 16-21). Their captivity and exile to foreign lands did not result simply because neighboring nations overpowered them. Rather, God uprooted them from their homeland as a result of their sin and rebellion against him. God's people not only defied him but also made him appear to conquering nations as weak and irresponsible as the gods those nations served. Thus the conquering nations had negative images of the God the Hebrew people supposedly served.[7]

Hence, verse 22 begins God's message to the Israelites about how he will restore the holiness of his name that has been profaned by his own people to the conquering nations. Interestingly enough, God declares that he will use the very people who defiled his name to repair his name among the nations. God will work in such a miraculous way with the Israelites that they will be transformed at the very depths of their being, offering a clear witness of God's work in them. God will gather his people from exile and restore them to the land he promised Abraham. Then God will cleanse them in a priestly washing to make them ceremonially clean, an act of worship with which the Israelites were familiar (v. 25).[8]

How can God solve the age-old problem with which the Israelites have suffered throughout their entire existence? That is, how can God work with them in such a way that they do not return to their familiar patterns of rebelliousness and sin, thus repeating their history of unfaithfulness? The answer lies in verses 26-27. Through yet another divine initiative, God will completely transform the hearts and lives of his people through re-creation. God promises that he will give his people "a new heart and put a new spirit" (v. 26) in them so that they may love and serve him

---

7. Brad E. Kelle, *Ezekiel*, New Beacon Bible Commentary (Kansas City: Beacon Hill Press of Kansas City, 2013), 296-97.

8. Ibid.

faithfully. Ezekiel hinted at this divine initiative in 11:19-20 and 18:31-32.[9] Ezekiel 36:25-28, then, explains God's transforming work more clearly.

We have the privilege of living twenty-five hundred years after God's promise to his people through Ezekiel. The Israelites certainly served God more faithfully following their return from exile. God never had to exile them again to foreign lands in order to return them to exclusive worship of him. However, we now know that God's promise to Ezekiel found a more complete fulfillment in the new covenant God brought his people through the incarnation of Jesus Christ. His life, example, ministry, death, and resurrection gave humanity a much clearer revelation of God than they had ever known. Add to that the coming of the Holy Spirit on the day of Pentecost into the hearts of waiting believers, and we see the reality God allowed Ezekiel briefly to see.

Verse 27 directly speaks of God putting his Spirit in us. It also challenges us to think at a deeper level about what God means when he says he will move us to follow his decrees and keep his laws. What does he mean by "move us"?[10] Some interpret this by saying he exercises divine sovereignty over us and forces us to live in ways that please him. Others (including me) believe the motivating force behind the word "move" references a perfect love infused in us by the precious, indwelling Holy Spirit, who compels us to serve him, not by force, but by a deep and abiding love that he gives us.[11] Take for example the loving act of Mary as she poured an expensive perfume on Jesus's feet and

---

9. See also Deuteronomy 30:6-8 and Psalm 51:10.
10. Kelle, *Ezekiel*, 297-99.
11. These two views highlight an important theological distinction. The first view, appealing to divine sovereignty, implies a determinism that violates human free will. The second view allows God to respect human free will and lead us in paths of righteousness by the power of his perfect love.

wiped them with her hair (John 12:3). An undivided love, not divine force, compelled Mary to honor Jesus in this most unusual way.

A testimony from early church history offers another powerful example of God's transforming love leading to faithful obedience. John was the last remaining disciple of Jesus in the early church. Polycarp (ca. AD 69–ca. AD 155), a student of John, bridged the transition between believers who experienced the incarnation of Christ and the first generation of believers following John's death. Polycarp lived in an era of intense persecution against the Christian faith. The Roman emperor demanded that all subjects declare that Caesar is Lord. Polycarp, along with many other Christians, refused to declare anything other than that Jesus is Lord. Roman authorities arrested him and offered him several opportunities to recant his faith in Christ. His testimony remains to this day a witness to the reality of God's perfect love indwelling the hearts of his disciples, leading to an undivided loyalty. Polycarp said, "For eighty-six years I have been his servant, and he has done me no wrong. How can I blaspheme my King who saved me?"[12] He died that day rather than betray Christ's love for him.

Simon Peter preached a powerful message when the Holy Spirit filled the disciples in the upper room on the day of Pentecost. He realized this gift of God's presence in believers' hearts fulfilled a prophecy of Joel, which he quoted: "In the last days, God says, I will pour out my Spirit on all people. Your sons and daughters will prophesy, your young men will see visions, your old men will dream dreams. Even on my servants, both men and women, I will pour out my Spirit in those days, and they will prophesy" (Acts

---

12. "The Martyrdom of Polycarp," in *The Apostolic Fathers*, trans. J. B. Lightfoot and J. R. Harmer, 2nd ed., ed. Michael W. Holmes (Grand Rapids: Baker, 1989), 139.

God revealed God's self progressively across the generations as he journeyed with Abraham and his descendants. The Old Testament offers a bird's-eye view of that journey.

2:17-18; Joel 2:28-29). Joel offers another example of Old Testament prophets looking forward to the day when God's Spirit would not simply be *with* his people but would abide *in* them. After the Holy Spirit appeared to the disciples waiting patiently for ten days as Jesus instructed them to do (Acts 1:4-5), Peter realized that the movement of God's Spirit "purify[ing] their hearts by faith" (15:8-9) was exactly what God told Joel would happen in God's perfect timing. Peter's sermon makes a natural transition in this conversation as we move from discussing the Holy Spirit being *with* believers in the Old Testament to being *in* them in the New Testament.

Examples of God's Spirit *in* Believers in the New Testament

God revealed God's self progressively across the generations as he journeyed with Abraham and his descendants. The Old Testament offers a bird's-eye view of that journey. The Israelites acknowledged the presence of God with them in a variety of ways throughout the Old Testament. Jacob encountered God as he wrestled with a man all night at Peniel (Gen. 32:22-32). Moses met with God through a burning bush that was not consumed (Exod. 3:1-22). God revealed his presence in a "cloud by day" and a "pillar of fire by night" as he traveled with the Hebrew slaves fleeing Egypt (13:21-22).

God knew that the fleeing slaves needed a location to gather for worship and to be reminded of the constant presence of God traveling with them. So God tasked Bezalel and Oholiab with building the tabernacle, as discussed earlier in this chapter. The people learned about God's holiness as the priests taught them the purpose of the Holy Place and the holy of holies in the tabernacle. The tabernacle traveled with the Israelites as they journeyed across the desert to the promised land.

Once the Israelites settled in the land God gave them, the need arose for a permanent building to serve as a center for worship. In time, Solomon constructed the temple. It, too, contained a Holy Place and a holy of holies. God's people remembered that God's presence dwelt with them every time they visited the temple. In his final extended conversation with the disciples recorded in John 14–16, Jesus revealed that God's presence would soon reside not just in a worship center like the temple but also within the hearts of believers. This reality identifies another difference between the old covenant between God and humanity and the new one.

In that final extended conversation, Jesus expanded the minds of his disciples beyond anything they had encountered in the past three years of following him. Much of what Jesus told them that night in the upper room made little sense until after his resurrection and the infilling of the Holy Spirit on the day of Pentecost. Notice some of the clues Jesus gave his disciples that night about the Holy Spirit coming to live *in* them.

Chapter 2 of this book explored the Christian understanding of the Trinity. Jesus called attention to the Trinity while instructing his disciples in John 14:16-17: "And *I* [Jesus] will ask the *Father*, and he will give you *another advocate* [Holy Spirit] to help you and be with you forever—the Spirit of Truth" (emphasis added). This awareness is essential to understanding how God dwells within believers. Jesus went on to say, "The world cannot accept him, because it neither sees him nor knows him. But you know him, for he lives with you and will be *in you*" (v. 17; emphasis added).

Then Jesus must have blown the disciples' minds when he connected the coming of the Holy Spirit into their hearts with the presence of the Father and himself in them. "On that day you will realize that I am in the Father, and you are in me, and I am in you" (v. 20). So when the Holy Spirit comes to live within the disciples of Jesus, they will also have the presence of the living Christ and the Father because Christ is in the Father.

Jesus expanded that thought with more detail as he continued: "Anyone who loves me will obey my teaching. My Father will love them, and we will come to them and make our home with them" (v. 23). Jesus made it clear that the presence of God (Father, Son, and Holy Spirit), recognized in the Holy Place and holy of holies of the tabernacle and temple in the Old Testament, now makes his "home" within the hearts of believers. God is not just with us as a protective parent but also at home in us! Augustine, one of the early church fathers in the fifth century, said of this passage of Scripture, "The Holy Spirit also makes a dwelling with the Father and the Son; he is at home in every way, like God in his temple. The God of the Trinity, the Father, the Son and the Holy Spirit, come to us when we come to them."[13]

Jesus inserted a few additional clues to this divine mystery as he continued the conversation with his disciples. He said, "In a little while you will see me no more, and then after a little while you will see me" (John 16:16). The most obvious fulfillment of this statement occurred when the disciples lost sight of Jesus following his crucifixion and burial. Then they saw him again in his visits with them during the time between his resurrection and ascension. Some commentators hold that Jesus might also have been referring to a spiritual sighting of himself through the ministry of the Holy Spirit as he taught them more about their Savior.

In the last recorded extended prayer of Jesus prior to his arrest, Jesus prayed, "I have given them the glory that you gave me, that they may be one as we are one—I in them and you in me—so that they may be brought to com-

---

13. George Lyons and T. Scott Daniels, *John 13–21*, New Beacon Bible Commentary (Kansas City: Beacon Hill Press of Kansas City, 2020), 86.

plete unity. Then the world will know that you sent me and have loved them even as you have loved me" (17:22-23). What a powerful thought: the unity of Christ's followers, then and now, mirrors the unity enjoyed by the members of the Holy Trinity! Notice again that short but potent phrase "I in them and you in me." Again, we watch a brief glimpse of the Holy Spirit bringing to us the presence of the living Christ, who, in turn, bears the presence of the Father. Jesus concluded this prayer with another reference to his presence within his disciples: "I have made you known to them, and will continue to make you known in order that the love you have for me may be in them and *that I myself may be in them*" (v. 26; emphasis added).

Jesus offers us in John 14–17 the most complete picture of God's self-revelation to humanity since Adam and Eve lived in the garden of Eden. He taught not only about the coming of the Holy Spirit but also about our connection to the love and unity that exists between the members of the Trinity, Father, Son, and Holy Spirit. The rest of the New Testament continues to expand our understanding of God abiding within our hearts and working through us as followers of Jesus Christ. We will discuss many of these insights in later chapters. For now, let's consider Paul's imagery of how God is not simply with us in a general sense but within us by his Spirit.

Modern psychology has taught us to think of ourselves from a variety of vantage points. For example, we often say a person is made up of a body, mind, soul, and spirit. Hebrew thought in the Bible knew nothing of such distinctions. The Hebrew people thought of humans as unitary beings, the parts of which cannot be separated. So for Paul, the spiritual indwelling of the Holy Spirit in the heart of a disciple included not only his or her spirit but every part of the disciple's being. He asked believers in the Corinthian church, "Do you not know that your bodies are temples of the Holy Spirit, who is *in you*, whom you have received from God?" (1 Cor. 6:19; emphasis added). Later, Paul asked these believers a similar question, "What agreement is there between the temple of God and idols? For we are the temple of the living God. As God has said: 'I will live with them and walk among them, and I will be their God, and they will be my people'" (2 Cor. 6:16). Paul also admonished his disciple Timothy: "Guard the good deposit that was entrusted to you—guard it with the help of *the Holy Spirit who lives in us*" (2 Tim. 1:14; emphasis added).

The Radical Difference

We cannot overemphasize the radical difference that exists between the old covenant and the new one in salvation history as the Holy Spirit makes the transition from being with believers to being in them. The promises and prophecies of the Old Testament prophets looked ahead to the days of the new covenant and marveled. We must never take for granted the blessing we enjoy as we live in the age of the Holy Spirit indwelling the hearts of believers. Having the Holy Spirit with us is a good thing; having him in us is better!

Words to Describe the Holy Spirit

1. Spirit of the Lord
2. Empowering
3. Indwelling

Questions for Reflection

1. Put in your own words the way you imagine the Holy Spirit working with Old Testament personalities such as Gideon, Samson, King Saul, and King David.

2. Why did the Holy Spirit give hints throughout the Old Testament about the coming Messiah?

3. If you lived in the days of Jeremiah, how would you have visualized God putting his law in your mind and writing it on your heart?

4. If you lived in the days of Ezekiel, how would you have visualized God giving you a new heart and a new spirit?

5. If you lived in the days of Joel, how would you have visualized God pouring out his Spirit on all people?

6. What made the Holy Place and the holy of holies in both the tabernacle and temple such special places in the hearts and minds of the Hebrew people?

7. What do you see as the biggest difference between the Holy Spirit being *with* believers in the Old Testament and *in* believers in the church age?

FIVE

Immanuel

"The virgin will conceive and give birth to a son, and they will call him Immanuel" (which means "God with us").
—Matthew 1:23

I believe that Jesus of Nazareth was the Saviour of the world, the Messiah so long foretold; that, being anointed with the Holy Ghost, he was a Prophet, revealing to us the whole will of God; that he was a Priest, who gave himself a sacrifice for sin, and still makes intercession for transgressors; that he is a King, who has all power in heaven and in earth, and will reign till he has subdued all things to himself.
—John Wesley[1]

Backstage Preparation

Local pastors in churches surrounding our metropolitan area received a letter several years ago informing them that the Billy Graham Evangelistic Association planned to hold a citywide crusade in our area. Our pastor received one of those letters and quickly sprang into action. He informed our church board of his desire for our church members to participate in the evangelistic effort. I served on the church board and received a valuable education over the next several months in the detailed preparations required to successfully execute such a monumental undertaking.

---

1. Wesley, "A Letter to a Roman Catholic," in *Works of John Wesley*, 10:81.

Until that experience I had no idea so much planning went into hosting a Billy Graham crusade.

We quickly learned that the Graham preparation team knew what they were doing from past events. They had checklists and timelines for every aspect of the year's preparations. I agreed to serve as an usher and altar worker. So I attended regular meetings over the next several months to learn how to best fulfill my roles. I was surprised at the hundreds of volunteer workers needed to serve both backstage and at various locations around the stadium.

Following careful preparation, the date of the crusade arrived. Tens of thousands of individuals poured into the stadium for the service. Every portion of the worship service occurred without a hitch, and Billy Graham preached a powerful gospel message. Many found Christ as their personal Savior at the conclusion of the service. I think every volunteer involved in the event felt it was worth all of the commitment and preparation required.

The Big Picture

Reading through the Old Testament from Genesis to Malachi reminds us that the Bible reveals much more than the details of individual stories like the ones we learned in children's Sunday school classes. Many of us grew up attending those classes where we learned about Noah and the ark, Jonah and the large fish, Moses and the Red Sea, and David and Goliath. We mastered the details of each of these stories and the spiritual lessons they taught us. However, we can easily focus so much attention on single events that we miss the big picture of the Old Testament message. When we consider the overarching narrative, we realize that the Holy Spirit played an important role in that bigger picture. The individual stories work together to teach us about God's salvation plan for humanity.

Here is a possible way for you to think of the metanarrative of the Old Testament:

- God created Adam and Eve and placed them in the perfect environment in the garden of Eden.
- Adam and Eve used free will to break the one and only rule God gave them.
- Rather than calling off the entire idea of having people made in God's image with free will, God decided to institute a salvation plan for his children.
- God gave hope to Adam and Eve when he hinted at his plan in Genesis 3:15.
- The first couple's descendants multiplied and spread out across the earth as they fulfilled God's command to "be fruitful and increase in number" (Gen. 1:28).
- The example of Adam and Eve exercising self-will rather than obeying God's will quickly repeated itself with the couple's descendants: Cain killed Abel, Noah lived in a rebellious generation, individuals at the tower of Babel rebelled against God, and so on.
- God narrowed his attention from many nations to one man, Abram, whom God blessed as he raised up an entire nation from that man's descendants, who, in turn, were to bless the nations of the world with the news of God's incredible love for humanity.
- God worked faithfully with the Israelites across the years when they obeyed God and when they did not, when they represented God well to the world and when they did not, and when they cooperated with God in his mission to live in relationship with them and when they did not.
- The Holy Spirit worked with individuals throughout the history of the nation of Israel to draw them

God's original design in creation included an unhindered divine-human relationship between the Creator and his children. The fall thwarted that plan.

to him so they could participate in each developing stage of God's salvation plan for humanity.
- Throughout the history of God's long-suffering patience with the Israelites, the Holy Spirit spoke through the prophets with the announcement of the coming Messiah.

We often refer to the Bible as the self-revelation of God to humanity. This is certainly true. But we must never forget that it is also the unfolding of the divine plan of salvation for humanity. God's original design in creation included an unhindered divine-human relationship between the Creator and his children. The fall thwarted that plan. Therefore, much of Scripture from Genesis 4 onward narrates God's mission in restoring that relationship. That makes the last bullet point extremely important. God never wanted the Israelites to live without peace and hope. To that end, he sent prophets to bring peace and enliven hope that someday God would send a Messiah who would institute a new covenant between God and humanity. Let's now turn our attention to those prophets.

Spirit Hints about the Messiah

A recent entertainment trend consists of people getting together with friends or family members at an establishment that for a fee will lock them in what is known as an escape room. These people then work together to discover a series of clues in the room leading from one to another until they reach the final clue that unlocks the door that leads to their escape.

The Holy Spirit worked across the entire Old Testament era preparing the way for the Messiah to come and bring the new covenant of God's salvation to us. Much like the clues in the escape room, the Holy Spirit gave Old Testament prophets and other believers of that era clues about the identity, activity, and salvation this Messiah would bring. The sheer number of these clues is overwhelming. The following list barely scratches the surface of information about the coming Messiah.

As you read the verses of Scripture accompanying the clues, keep in mind that Old Testament prophecies often had three references of fulfillment: the current day or near future, the incarnation of Jesus Christ, and the end of time. Therefore, those who heard the prophecies sometimes derived meaning from current or near-future events. Those events, however, did not entirely explain the prophetic message. Jesus, the disciples, and the early church saw phrases or images in the prophecies clarified in the life, ministry, death, and resurrection of Jesus Christ. Even then, certain phrases and images remained unexplained. We still read those unexplained prophecies today through eyes of faith as we await the second coming. Here then are some of the prophetic hints the Holy Spirit gave the Old Testament prophets:

- He will come from the lineage of David (Jer. 23:5; Ps. 132:11;[2] Isa. 11:10).
- He will reign on King David's throne (Isa. 9:7).
- He will be born in Bethlehem (Mic. 5:2).
- He will be born as a child to a virgin (Isa. 9:6; 7:14).
- He will be called Immanuel, "God with us" (Isa. 7:14).
- He will establish God's kingdom forever (Dan. 2:44).
- He will bring a government and peace that will rule the world with justice and righteousness (Isa. 9:7).
- "He will bring justice to the nations" (Isa. 42:1).
- He will bring great light to the world (Isa. 9:2).

---

2. David and other psalm writers were not officially prophets, but many statements they made in the Psalms were recognized during the incarnation as references to the Messiah.

- He will be a leader and commander (Isa. 55:4).
- He will be a conqueror (Ps. 68:18).
- He will have dominion over the nations (Num. 24:19; Pss. 72:8; 110:2).
- He will judge the nations (Isa. 2:4).
- His enemies will become his footstool (Ps. 110:1).
- He will be "mighty to save" (Isa. 63:1).
- He will bring salvation to the ends of the earth (Isa. 49:6; 59:6; 62:11).
- He will be the cornerstone of God's kingdom (Isa. 28:16).
- He will lead worship as a priest (Ps. 110:4; Zech. 6:13).
- He will speak for God as a prophet (Deut. 18:15, 18).
- The "zeal of the LORD Almighty" will establish the rule of the Messiah (Isa. 9:7).

Jesus quoted many of these passages of Scripture as he preached and taught. We gain a feel for his ministry as we hear him recite Scripture from Isaiah 61:1-2, 58:6: "The Spirit of the Lord is on me, because he has anointed me to proclaim good news to the poor. He has sent me to proclaim freedom for the prisoners and recovery of sight for the blind, to set the oppressed free, to proclaim the year of the Lord's favor" (Luke 4:18-19).

Suffering Servant

Old Testament prophets also spoke of a Suffering Servant. They misunderstood an important connection at the time, as did those who listened to the preaching and teaching of Jesus Christ. However, following the crucifixion of Jesus on the cross, his disciples and members of the early church realized that Old Testament prophecies about the coming Messiah and Suffering Servant both referenced the incarnation of Jesus Christ. Here are a few prophecies about the Suffering Servant.

- He will be an exalted servant (Isa. 52:13).
- He will be disfigured so as not to be recognized as a human being (Isa. 52:14).
- He will be rejected like a stone rejected by builders (Ps. 118:22).
- He will be offered vinegar as he dies (Ps. 69:21).
- He will be called the Branch who will build the temple of the Lord (Zech. 3:8; 6:12).
- He will humbly ride into town on a donkey (Zech. 9:9).
- Thirty pieces of silver will be paid in a traitorous transaction (Zech. 11:12).
- He will be pierced as people mourn his death (Zech. 12:10).

The most complete prophecy of the Suffering Servant appears in Isaiah 53. The imagery cannot be summarized into fewer words. Here is the prophecy in its entirety:

Who has believed our message
    and to whom has the arm of the Lord been
        revealed?
He grew up before him like a tender shoot,
    and like a root out of dry ground.
He had no beauty or majesty to attract us to him,
    nothing in his appearance that we should desire
        him.
He was despised and rejected by mankind,
    a man of suffering, and familiar with pain.
Like one from whom people hide their faces
    he was despised, and we held him in low esteem.

Surely he took up our pain
    and bore our suffering,

yet we considered him punished by God,
> stricken by him, and afflicted.
But he was pierced for our transgressions,
> he was crushed for our iniquities;
the punishment that brought us peace was on him,
> and by his wounds we are healed.
We all, like sheep, have gone astray,
> each of us has turned to our own way;
and the Lord has laid on him
> the iniquity of us all.

He was oppressed and afflicted,
> yet he did not open his mouth;
he was led like a lamb to the slaughter,
> and as a sheep before its shearers is silent,
> so he did not open his mouth.
By oppression and judgment he was taken away.
> Yet who of his generation protested?
For he was cut off from the land of the living;
> for the transgression of my people he was
> > punished.
He was assigned a grave with the wicked,
> and with the rich in his death,
though he had done no violence,
> nor was any deceit in his mouth.

Yet it was the Lord's will to crush him and cause him
> > to suffer,
> and though the Lord makes his life an offering
> > for sin,
he will see his offspring and prolong his days,
> and the will of the Lord will prosper in his hand.
After he has suffered,
> he will see the light of life and be satisfied;
by his knowledge my righteous servant will justify
> > many,

> and he will bear their iniquities.
> Therefore I will give him a portion among the great,
> > and he will divide the spoils with the strong,
> because he poured out his life unto death,
> > and was numbered with the transgressors.
> For he bore the sin of many,
> > and made intercession for the transgressors. (Isa. 53:1-12)

People sometimes ask why teachers of the law and religious scholars in the Old Testament era did not connect prophecies of the coming Messiah with those of the Suffering Servant. Part of the answer to that question may lie in preconceived notions and expectations. Remember that the Hebrew people lived in subjection to enemy nations or regional empires for much of their existence. Only from the golden age of King David's rule to the failing days of the divided kingdom did they experience civil independence. A brief period following the rebellion of the Maccabees (167-134 BC) also gave them a measure of freedom.

For that reason, prophecies related to their coming Messiah conjured images of civil and political independence from conquering nations. These images brought hope of a mighty conqueror who would crush their enemies and establish a political kingdom that would finally bring their national dreams to reality. We hear that hope following Jesus's resurrection and just prior to his ascension to heaven. Jesus's disciples asked him, "Lord, are you at this time going to restore the kingdom to Israel?" (Acts 1:6).

Because Old Testament prophecies referred to the Messiah coming from the lineage of King David, hearers assumed their Messiah would restore the golden age of David. They could not possibly imagine a connection between prophecies about the conquering Messiah and those of the Suffering Servant. They could not imagine these prophecies referring to the same person. Not until the ministry of the early church as highlighted in the book of Acts did Jesus's followers fully realize that he brought a spiritual kingdom to earth and that his death on the cross occupied a central place in the gospel message about their Messiah. Before we move on to another subject, we need to look at the life and ministry of an additional Old Testament prophet.

Then Came John

I learned about the importance of timely reminders while teaching university students. I always gave them a copy of the course syllabus on the first day of class. The syllabus contained the objectives, expectations, and assignments for the course and due dates for each assignment. I read important portions of the syllabus to the entire class, gave particular attention to the due dates, and asked if anyone had questions about the expectations. Despite my efforts on the first day, I still found it necessary to remind students along the way about due dates for term papers and exams. I especially emphasized expectations and due dates for any final projects.

Perhaps providing such a timely reminder is one of the reasons God sent a prophet at the end of the Old Testament era. He wanted to reignite interest in prophecies about the coming Messiah and prepare people for the Messiah's arrival. Most of these prophecies came to the Israelites hundreds of years earlier. Much happened in the intervening years. Generations passed. Cultures and customs changed. People needed a last-minute reminder.

The last Old Testament prophet preparing the way for the Messiah was John the Baptist. We know the Holy Spirit used him in an unusual way because when the angel of the Lord announced John's coming to his father Zechariah, the angel said, "He will be filled with the Holy Spirit even before he is born" (Luke 1:15). The Holy Spirit empowered John in the same way God's Spirit worked *with* individuals to accomplish a particular divine assignment in the Old Testament. It is not the same as being filled with the Holy Spirit on the day of Pentecost and in the church age.

John the Baptist was a most unusual prophet. We believe that due to their extended age his parents probably died while he was a young child. Pious believers known as Essenes lived separate from the larger society in the desert. Luke said, "He lived in the wilderness until he appeared publicly to Israel" (v. 80). Guardians taught John the Hebrew faith and prepared him for the ministry to which the Holy Spirit called him.

John the Baptist caught people's attention as he began his public ministry. He wore rough clothing made of camel's hair; he ate a primitive diet of locust and wild honey. He proclaimed a powerful message of repentance and forgiveness of sins in preparation for the coming Messiah. Luke said he fulfilled the prophetic words of Isaiah 40:3-5, which begins, "A voice of one calling in the wilderness, 'Prepare the way for the Lord, make straight paths for him'" (Luke 3:4). Many heard John's message, repented of their sins, and waited expectantly for the coming Messiah.

John always understood his life and ministry in relation to the one who was to come. He bridged the gap between the old covenant and the new one. He prepared the way for the Messiah's coming, baptized him, and then faded from public view. He said of his relationship to Jesus, "He must become greater; I must become less" (John 3:30). John also understood differences in their ministries. He said, "I baptize you with water for repentance. But after me comes one who is more powerful than I, whose sandals I am not worthy to carry. He will baptize you with the Holy Spirit and fire. His winnowing fork is in his hand, and he will clear his threshing floor, gathering his wheat into the barn and burning up the chaff with unquenchable fire"

(Matt. 3:11-12). We will discuss the meaning of Jesus's baptism "with the Holy Spirit and fire" in a future chapter.

John the Baptist's public ministry ended with his imprisonment by Herod just as Jesus's public ministry began. Their central messages were much the same: repent of your sins in preparation for the coming kingdom. Yet something was different. This transition between the ministries of John and Jesus highlights the transition between God's old covenant with humanity and his new one. John sent a question from prison through one of his disciples to Jesus: "Are you the one who is to come, or should we expect someone else?" (Matt. 11:3). John may have been discouraged in his prison cell, and Jesus's public ministry might not have been as dramatic as he expected. We don't know exactly what prompted his question. Jesus offered evidence that the prophecy of Isaiah 35:5-6 found fulfillment in his public ministry. God was bringing transformation and healing to those in need.

As John's disciples returned to prison to relay Jesus's response to John's question, Jesus gave John a very insightful commendation. He first affirmed that the ministry of John fulfilled the prophecy of Malachi 3:1 and 4:5 that the ministry of Elijah (2 Kings 1:7-8) would precede the Messiah's arrival. Jesus did not criticize John for his prison doubts. Rather, he said, "Truly I tell you, among those born of women there has not risen anyone greater than John the Baptist" (Matt. 11:11). But Jesus did not stop there. He went on to say something astounding: "Yet whoever is least in the kingdom of heaven is greater than he" (v. 11).

Before considering what Jesus meant by that statement, let's examine four important passages of Scripture. In 2 Corinthians 3:7-18 Paul compared and contrasted the old covenant with the new one. He pointed to all of the limitations of the old one and the advantages of the new one. He specifically called attention to the work of the Holy Spirit in the new covenant: "Now the Lord is the Spirit, and where the Spirit of the Lord is, there is freedom. And we all, who with unveiled faces contemplate the Lord's glory, are being transformed into his image with ever-increasing glory, which comes from the Lord, who is the Spirit" (vv. 17-18).

A second important passage of Scripture comes from the book of Hebrews:

> In the past God spoke to our ancestors through the prophets at many times and in various ways, but in these last days he has spoken to us by his Son, whom he appointed heir of all things, and through whom also he made the universe. The Son is the radiance of God's glory and the exact representation of his being, sustaining all things by his powerful word. After he had provided purification for sins, he sat down at the right hand of the Majesty in heaven. (1:1-3)

Later, the writer says, "But in fact the ministry Jesus has received is as superior to theirs as the covenant of which he is mediator is superior to the old one, since the new covenant is established on better promises" (8:6).

Finally, Jesus said as he instructed his disciples, "For truly I tell you, many prophets and righteous people longed to see what you see but did not see it, and to hear what you hear but did not hear it" (Matt. 13:17). Considering these four passages of Scripture together, we see what Jesus meant by, "Yet whoever is least in the kingdom of heaven is greater than he [John the Baptist]" (11:11). John, the last Old Testament prophet, anticipated the coming Messiah through the hints given by the Holy Spirit across hundreds of years. No Old Testament prophet could put all of the clues together to see the big picture of the new covenant. But, and this is really significant, the young children in our Sunday school classes today know more about God's incredible plan of salvation through the life, ministry, death, and resurrection of Jesus Christ than did any Old Testament prophet! Peter explained it like this,

> Concerning this salvation, the prophets, who spoke of the grace that was to come to you, searched intently and with the greatest care, trying to find out the time and circumstances to which the Spirit of Christ in them was pointing when he predicted the sufferings of the Messiah and the glories that would follow. It was revealed to them that they were not serving themselves but you, when they spoke of the things that have now been told you by those who have preached the gospel to you by the Holy Spirit sent from heaven. Even angels long to look into these things. (1 Pet. 1:10-12)

Paul added, "The mystery that has been kept hidden for ages and generations, but is now disclosed to the Lord's people. To them God has chosen to make known among the Gentiles the glorious riches of this mystery, which is Christ in you, the hope of glory" (Col. 1:26-27).

There Were Others

Before we end this discussion of Immanuel, we should look at two other Old Testament personalities briefly mentioned at the birth of Jesus. His birth took place privately with Mary and Joseph in an animal shelter in Bethlehem. They received their first confirmation that the newborn baby was the long-awaited Messiah when shepherds from a nearby field arrived to announce that an angel of the Lord had told them the Messiah had arrived and invited them to go see for themselves (Luke 2:8-18). When the shepherds left the animal shelter, they told everyone what they had seen and heard.

Eight days later, Joseph and Mary took their newborn to the temple in Jerusalem to present him to the Lord. Here, for the first time, two ordinary people proclaimed in this very public place that the Messiah was in the building. First,

Simeon testified to the Messiah's presence because the Holy Spirit was with him and had promised that he would meet the Messiah before he died and had directed him to visit the temple at just the right time. Simeon was the only person in the Bible to refer to Jesus as the "consolation of Israel" (v. 25) and the "Lord's Christ" (v. 26, KJV). The message for his song of praise came from Isaiah 9:1-3; 42:6; 49:6; 51:4; 60:3. His testimony is the first in the book of Luke to declare that Jesus came to save both Jews and Gentiles.

Immediately after Simeon proclaimed Jesus as the long-awaited Messiah, an elderly woman named Anna who worshipped daily at the temple approached Joseph and Mary. She, like Simeon, testified that the newborn was the Messiah. By this time in the fulfillment of the Old Testament prophets' promises of a coming Messiah a pattern begins to emerge. Zechariah and Elizabeth, parents of John the Baptist; Mary, mother of Jesus, and Joseph, husband of Mary; field hands tending a flock of sheep at night; elderly Simeon; widowed Anna—all share something in common. They are all quiet, simple, ordinary people to whom the world offered no honor or praise. Yet the Holy Spirit used each of them in unique ways to usher the Savior of the world into our presence. Thank God for quiet, simple, ordinary people!

Before we conclude this chapter, allow me to digress just a bit. We often refer to Hebrews 11 as the Hall of Fame of those who lived by faith. The chapter names many Old Testament personalities we expect to find: Noah, Abraham, Sarah, Isaac, Jacob, and Joseph, to name a few. Three words in verse 35, however, deserve a comment. After naming an impressive list of faithful believers, verse 35 begins with the words "There were others . . ." Every time I read those words I am reminded of a comment one of my professors made in graduate school. He said, "The Bible and church history record a number of individuals we know by name who accomplished a great deal for God and his kingdom. They get most of our attention. But never forget the countless number of nameless men and women who served the Lord faithfully throughout their lifetimes. The Holy Spirit worked through them as well; they passed the faith to us just as they received it. Only eternity will reveal the value of their faithfulness."[3]

So when I read the words "There were others . . . ," I remember how effectively the Holy Spirit worked in the lives of the countless number of nameless men and women who now participate in the "cloud of witnesses" cheering us toward the finish line (Heb. 12:1). They heard the prophecies of the coming Messiah. They exercised faith and hope in the God of those prophecies. And they lived their lives in anticipation of his arrival. Yes, praise him for Immanuel; God is with us!

Words to Describe the Holy Spirit

1. Planner
2. Enabler
3. Preparer

---

[3]. Herman Norton, Vanderbilt University class lecture, 1982.

Questions for Reflection

1. Recall a time when you participated in planning a big event. What details went into the preparation?

2. Why do you think Adam and Eve found it impossible to resist breaking the one and only rule God gave them?

3. Why do you think God decided to work with a redemption plan for humans rather than destroy them when they used their free will to rebel against him?

4. How does God's blessing in the lives of Abraham and Sarah offer you faith and hope for the way he works in your life?

5. Why do you think God continued to work with the nation of Israel after they rebelled against him again and again throughout the Old Testament?

6. Why did the religious scholars and teachers of the law in the Old Testament not realize that the prophecies about the coming Messiah and Suffering Servant referred to the same person?

7. Read Isaiah 53 again. What fulfillments of this prophecy do you see in the incarnation of Jesus Christ?

8. Why do you think John the Baptist is classified as an Old Testament prophet even though the story of his life and ministry are recorded in the New Testament?

9. How was the promise of the Messiah coming to earth better than the Ten Commandments in offering hope to the Hebrew people?

10. Name some of the individuals who made a positive impact on your spiritual journey but who never became famous or were considered noteworthy by society.

SIX | Incarnation

The Word became flesh and made his dwelling among us.
—John 1:14

The gospel, (that is, good tidings, good news for guilty, helpless sinners,) in the largest sense of the word, means, the whole revelation made to men by Jesus Christ; and sometimes the whole account of what our Lord did and suffered while he tabernacled among men.
—John Wesley[1]

Everything Changes

God blesses the journey of life with some incredible experiences. A married couple participates in one of the greatest blessings when news arrives that a baby is coming. Emotions soar with the anticipation, education, and preparation that go into welcoming a child into the family. Nine months seem like an eternity as the days pass slowly, especially if complications surface along the way. Great joy accompanies the arrival of the newborn, and just about everything in the family changes from that day forward. If you, your family members, or your friends have experienced the preparations for and arrival of a newborn, you know what I mean.

---

1. Wesley, "Sermon VII: The Way to the Kingdom," in *Works of John Wesley*, 5:84-85.

Everything changed in our world when the Messiah came to live with us.

Think for a few minutes about all the changes that take place from the time a couple learns of a pregnancy until the baby's birth. This reflection gives you a glimpse into what heaven experienced as the Holy Spirit brought the plan of sending the Messiah to earth from prediction to reality. Instead of nine months of preparation, the Holy Spirit worked for thousands of years to complete preparations for this earth-altering event. We have considered many of the preparations in the last three chapters. The entire story of God's relationship with humanity from the fall in Genesis 3 to the arrival of Jesus Christ in an animal shelter in Bethlehem entered into those preparations. When you have an opportunity, read the entire Old Testament. As you are meditating on the text and listening to the Spirit, ask yourself, "How does this relate to the Holy Spirit's work in bringing the Messiah to our world?" You will be amazed as you put each day's reading into the context of God's plan of salvation for us by sending the Messiah.

Just as everything changes when a newborn comes to live in a family, everything changed in our world when the Messiah came to live with us. John wrote, "The Word became flesh and made his dwelling among us" (John 1:14). The words translated "made his dwelling among us" literally mean he "tabernacled among us" or "pitched his tent among us." The popular television program *Undercover Boss* illustrates this well. In each episode, the president of a large corporation leaves his or her spacious office, puts on work clothes, and works side by side with everyday laborers in the company. The president discovers firsthand what workers do, how they feel, and how he or she can improve the work experience of the employees.

There are some differences between what the corporate executive does on a television program and what Jesus Christ did in coming to our world. The undercover boss masquerades as a common laborer; Jesus is the actual Son of Man.

The corporate executive is an ordinary human being just like the company laborers. Jesus Christ left the glory and majesty of heaven along with the worship due him as the second person of the holy Trinity to come to our world and experience life on earth as a human being. Paul stated it well when he said of Jesus Christ, "Who, being in very nature God, did not consider equality with God something to be used to his own advantage; rather, he made himself nothing by taking the very nature of a servant, being made in human likeness. And being found in appearance as a man, he humbled himself by becoming obedient to death—even death on a cross!" (Phil. 2:6-8). The corporate executive returned to his spacious office at the conclusion of the television program. The entire experience consumed only a few days. Jesus lived among us for thirty-three years and then gave his life on the cross for our salvation.

Promises Fulfilled

The previous chapters of this book have attempted a brief overview of God's salvation plan for humanity as executed by the Holy Spirit, the third person of the Trinity. In the last chapter, we brought many Old Testament prophecies together and highlighted them in light of the ministry of the last Old Testament prophet John the Baptist. The ministry of John the Baptist briefly overlapped the ministry of Jesus Christ, most notably when John baptized Jesus in the Jordan River.

This chapter will give attention to the work of the Holy Spirit in the life, ministry, teaching, death, resurrection, and ascension of Jesus Christ. Much more is said of the incarnation of Jesus in books addressing the various aspects of his time on earth. The theological series in which this book belongs also has a volume specifically dedicated to Jesus Christ. The previous chapter presented numerous prophecies by Old Testament prophets about the coming

Messiah and the Suffering Servant. We will not attempt to find specific fulfillments of each prophecy. That undertaking would fill an entire book in itself. If you are interested in learning more about Christ's fulfillment of these Old Testament prophecies, you can consult a study Bible or a chain-reference Bible. It is worth the time and attention to learn how completely Jesus fulfilled Old Testament prophecies about the coming Messiah and the Suffering Servant.

An Important Introduction

As we observed above, the ministries of John the Baptist and Jesus intersected at the baptism of Jesus. John objected strongly when Jesus asked to be baptized by him. John knew that Jesus was the Messiah and did not need to be baptized as evidence of repentance and the forgiveness of sins in order to be restored to a right relationship with God the Father. Jesus insisted, however, so John honored his request.

Much more took place at this sacred ceremony than simply getting Jesus wet in the Jordan River. This event carries great significance for New Testament believers because it is our first introduction to the Trinity. This concept became a major stumbling block for Jewish religious leaders. In their minds, the idea of Trinity violated the declaration of Deuteronomy 6:4: "Hear, O Israel: The LORD our God, the LORD is one." If God is one, how could he relate to us as two persons—one in heaven and one on earth? For New Testament believers, on the other hand, this high and holy moment offered evidence that our God is Father, Son, and Holy Spirit, in Trinity. Matthew recounted the event like this: "As soon as Jesus was baptized, he went up out of the water. At that moment heaven was opened, and he saw the Spirit of God descending like a dove and alighting on him. And a voice from heaven said, 'This is my Son, whom I love; with him I am well pleased'" (Matt. 3:16-17).

John needed to baptize Jesus for several important reasons. First, it fulfilled the divine law (5:17). Next, it marked the transition from the old dispensation of the law to the new dispensation of mercy and grace. Third, it gave God the opportunity to reveal the concept of the Trinity to our world. Fourth, it marked the commissioning of Jesus into public ministry. Fifth, it gave the Father a chance to acknowledge Jesus as his Son. Sixth, onlookers saw that the Holy Spirit blessed Jesus and would be assisting in Jesus's ministry. And finally, it marked the beginning of a new approach to humanity's salvation through the provisions of the new covenant.[2]

An Important Test

In the Christian journey, mountaintop spiritual experiences that draw us near to the heart of God often precede periods of testing. Such is the case with Jesus immediately following his baptism. Mark reports, "At once the Spirit sent him out into the wilderness" (Mark 1:12).[3] Luke put it like this, "Jesus, full of the Holy Spirit, left the Jordan and *was led by the Spirit* into the wilderness" (Luke 4:1; emphasis added).

Why, you ask, would the Holy Spirit lead Jesus to a place of severe temptation? Part of the answer may lie in Paul's comparison between Adam and Jesus:

> So it is written: "The first man Adam became a living being"; the last Adam [Jesus], a life-giving spirit. The spiritual did not come first, but the natural, and after that the spiritual. The first man was of the dust of the earth; the second man is of heaven. As was the earthly man, so are those who are of the earth; and as is the

---

2. Carter, *Person and Ministry*, 101-2.
3. In Mark the Greek literally says the Spirit "cast him out into the wilderness."

heavenly man, so also are those who are of heaven. And just as we have borne the image of the earthly man, so shall we bear the image of the heavenly man. (1 Cor. 15:45-49)

The first Adam failed to resist the serpent's temptation. With that failure came moral depravity and a broken relationship with Creator God for all humanity. A bent toward self-will entered the heart of every person born to the first Adam's race. Satan usurped an earthly authority as individuals from that time onward made willful decisions to disobey God, reject divine authority, and please themselves.

Jesus, the last Adam, had to face temptation head-on and defeat Satan by refusing to surrender to him. The second temptation of Jesus illustrates this clearly. The devil showed Jesus all the kingdoms of the world and then claimed he could give them to Jesus because they were his (Luke 4:5-7). Does that mean the devil had a title deed to all the kingdoms of this world? Absolutely not! Humans give the devil power and authority by yielding to temptation. The devil can only suggest; humans use their will bent toward the self to make decisions that give the devil control in the lives of all who yield. Jesus refused to yield to the devil's temptations and in so doing won the victory over the devil. Jesus accomplished something people did not believe could be done; he said no to the devil by the power of the Holy Spirit.

In the Power of the Spirit

Luke said that "Jesus returned to Galilee in the power of the Spirit" (Luke 4:14) following his wilderness battles with the devil. That phrase "in the power of the Spirit" characterizes everything about the life, teaching, and preaching ministry of Jesus. We spoke in chapter 2 about the symbiotic relationship between the members of the holy Trinity. Some Bible teachers read a passage of Scripture from either the Old or New Testament and say, "Here we see the ministry of God the Father," or "This is the work of the Son." It's unlikely that anyone on earth has the spiritual insight to attribute an event solely to one member of the Trinity. Scripture seems to teach us that while the Father, Son, or Spirit may be identified with a particular event, all members of the Trinity function together in ways that we may not fully understand.

Prophecy Fulfilled

Jesus's public ministry began with him teaching in synagogues throughout Galilee. He then made his way to his hometown of Nazareth for the official announcement of his ministry's focus on the poor and needy. Local people knew him well, since they had observed him in worship services and interactions in the community throughout his childhood. On one particular Sabbath, Jesus attended the synagogue of his childhood. The leader invited him to speak and handed him the scroll of Scripture. He read from the book of Isaiah and called attention to two passages: 61:1-2 and 58:6.

> The Spirit of the Lord is on me,
>> because he has anointed me
>> to proclaim good news to the poor.
> He has sent me to proclaim freedom for the prisoners
>> and recovery of sight for the blind,
> to set the oppressed free,
>> to proclaim the year of the Lord's favor. (Luke 4:18-19)

Notice that Luke's quotation from Isaiah 61:1-2 stops in the middle of verse 2. This is significant because it calls attention to the focus of Jesus's earthly ministry. Verse 18 speaks of the compassion he will have as he proclaims good news to the poor, prisoners, blind, and oppressed. The first section of verse 19 speaks of the Lord's favor. Notice the hope in this portion from Isaiah. The next phrase in Isaiah 61:2 says the Messiah will proclaim "the day of vengeance of our God." Jesus wanted his hearers to know that the good news of the gospel contained hope and healing, not judgment.[4]

After reading from the Isaiah passages, Jesus referenced two particular events from the ministries of two highly regarded Old Testament prophets. He called particular attention to Elijah ministering to the physical needs of a Gentile woman during an extended drought (1 Kings 17:8-24) and Elisha instructing Naaman, a Gentile leper, for God's healing (2 Kings 5:1-19). As with these two great prophets, Jesus came to bring good news not only to Jews but also to Gentiles. What a shocking revelation for God's chosen people to digest about their Messiah!

Worshippers who heard Jesus speak in synagogues in other villages prior to this day liked his message and shared positive comments with their friends about him. It was not so in his hometown. The rejection of his message and ministry in Nazareth foreshadowed the rejection of many others as he traveled throughout Israel. As in these early days of ministry, some welcomed his message; others did not. This rejection foreshadowed another reaction to come in future days: his death. They actually wanted to kill him. Jesus must have felt great pain because of the rejection he received from the residents of his hometown, a small village of about four hundred residents.[5] Perhaps it was too much for local residents to believe that the Spirit of the Lord could anoint the ministry of Jesus as Isaiah prophesied. Yet Luke believed that is exactly what Jesus was proclaiming right before their eyes. The Spirit of God was bringing the

---

4. David A. Neale, *Luke 1–9*, New Beacon Bible Commentary (Kansas City: Beacon Hill Press of Kansas City, 2011), 121.
5. Ibid., 118.

prophecies of Isaiah to life in their midst. However, their familiarity with this child of the community blinded them to his divine reality.

Assumed Not Stated

All three authors of the Synoptic Gospels include an account of Jesus returning to Nazareth to preach in his hometown (Matt. 13:54-58; Mark 6:1-6; Luke 4:14-30). All three highlight his rejection from the local worshipping community. Only Luke includes the reading from Isaiah 61:1-2, which began with "The Spirit of the Lord is on me" (Luke 4:18). We might expect that the Synoptic authors would call frequent attention to the work of the Holy Spirit in the preaching, teaching, and miracle-working ministry of Jesus. However, this is not the case. The authors make almost no mention of the Spirit's empowerment in Jesus's ministry. I conclude from this that the authors assumed that after the visual image of the dove descending on Jesus at his baptism (and for Luke the added account of the declaration from Isaiah's prophecy), everything Jesus said and did in ministry was empowered by the Holy Spirit.

One passage in Luke's Gospel deserves special attention, since it is a notable exception to the assumption just mentioned. In Luke 11 Jesus taught his disciples how to pray. Verses 2-4 summarize what we know today as the Lord's Prayer. Jesus then gave an extended illustration and comment on the importance of persistence in prayer. He concluded his insight with these words: "Which of you fathers, if your son asks for a fish, will give him a snake instead? Or if he asks for an egg, will give him a scorpion? If you then, though you are evil, know how to give good gifts to your children, how much more will your Father in heaven give the Holy Spirit to those who ask him!" (vv. 11-13).

This is a profound passage of Scripture for at least two reasons. First, it is one of the few times Jesus talks direct-

God invites us to pray persistently to be filled with his Holy Spirit.

ly to his disciples or audiences about the Holy Spirit. And second, it is the first time Jesus promised his disciples that the day was coming when they would be empowered by the Holy Spirit. Jesus used a common Jewish teaching tool of the day; he told a "how much more" story. Certainly if a child asked an earthly father for a fish or an egg, he would not respond with a snake or a scorpion. How much more, then, would God respond with good gifts for his children? God is the source of all love and compassion. The best father known to humanity would be considered evil when compared with the love and compassion of our God.

But Jesus was not talking about us requesting fish or eggs. Rather, he is introducing his disciples to the grandest of all prayer requests: to be filled with the Holy Spirit. For the first time, Jesus indicated to his disciples that God the Father was not reserving the power of the Holy Spirit for the life and ministry of Jesus alone. He instead wanted his disciples to begin thinking about the possibility that they, too, could pray to be empowered by the Spirit. What's more, God longs to grant this request in the same way as parents love to give good gifts to their children. Notice Jesus describes the Holy Spirit as a gift from God.[6]

This conversation between Jesus and his disciples sets the stage in the disciples' hearts and minds for the vivid details Jesus will give them on his last night with them (John 14–16) and the empowerment of the Holy Spirit they will receive on the day of Pentecost (Acts 2:1-4). This conversation is the only time in Luke's Gospel where Jesus indicates that his disciples can receive the gift of the Holy Spirit. God says he wants to bestow his Spirit on all who believe in Christ. "It is a passage in which the quest for sanctification finds particular scriptural warrant. Only here in the Gospel

---

6. David A. Neale, *Luke 9–24*, New Beacon Bible Commentary (Kansas City: Beacon Hill Press of Kansas City, 2013), 79.

traditions are we encouraged to persistently seek the bequest of the Holy Spirit."[7]

Within the context of this powerful announcement by Jesus, he gives his disciples at least three insights to mentally process. First, God invites us to pray persistently to be filled with his Holy Spirit. Second, we must depend completely on God for the answer to that prayer. Third, our loving heavenly Father wants to grant our request for the fullness of the Spirit within us even more than we understand our need for him. John Wesley noted the progression in the story from a discussion about a friend to an earthly father to our heavenly Father.[8]

Easter Eggs and Bread Crumbs

Technology companies often employ an effective marketing technique to pique the interest of potential buyers of a new product. They put "Easter eggs" in television commercials, social media ads, or print magazines. That is, they drop hints about new and exciting features coming to the latest cell phone, smart television, or satellite receiver. Previous versions of this technique, known as leaving bread crumbs, left small clues across a wide array of information outlets to whet consumer appetites for upcoming products. Easter eggs and bread crumbs work; just look at the long lines at stores on the morning a new electronic product hits the market.

We saw Jesus use a similar technique to teach his disciples in Luke 11:11-13. He wanted them to begin thinking about the possibility of being filled with the Holy Spirit. Jesus wanted that possibility to grow and develop in their hearts and minds so that when the time came, they would wait for the promise of the Father (Acts 1:4). This was not

---

7. Ibid., 80.
8. Carter, *Person and Ministry*, 106.

Just as the Spirit blew to bring about physical life on the day of our creation, he now blows to bring about spiritual life when we are born again.

the only time Jesus dropped hints about the infilling of the Holy Spirit. John offers several additional examples. Let's take a quick look at them.

In John 3, Jesus employed a unique image and a play on words as he taught Nicodemus (vv. 1-15). First, Jesus described the entrance into the kingdom of God with the unique image of an adult being born again. Only in John do we see the parallel between being born into the world with physical life and being born again with spiritual life. Nicodemus misunderstood Jesus's meaning at first because the concept was so novel to him. We must experience both births to be citizens of the kingdom Jesus described here. Scholars offer a variety of opinions explaining the meaning of the need to be "born of water and the Spirit" (v. 5). The simplest explanation compares physical birth to the water surrounding a baby in its mother's womb and spiritual birth to the Holy Spirit granting spiritual life in the new birth.

Second, Jesus employed a play on words that carried profound insight into the work of the Holy Spirit in our lives. He compared the work of the Spirit in our new birth to the wind blowing. This makes sense; we cannot see the Spirit or the wind move, but we can see the effect of the movement. Jesus implied a deeper meaning, however. We described the work of the Holy Spirit in chapter 3 of this book as he bent over the lifeless form of Adam and lovingly blew into his nostrils the breath of life. In that moment "the man became a living being" (Gen. 2:7). The wordplay between the wind and the Holy Spirit suggests that just as the Spirit blew to bring about physical life on the day of our creation, he now blows to bring about spiritual life when we are born again.

John dropped another hint about the Holy Spirit in John 3:34. We could easily conclude that God loves his Son infinitely because his Son is sinless and God always works mightily through him. We have no problem believing that.

We might, however, have a problem believing that he loves us no less because of our sinful past and frequent tendency to make mistakes. John 3:16 states, "For God so loved the world that he gave his one and only Son, that whoever believes in him shall not perish but have eternal life." That eternal life comes from the life-giving Holy Spirit. John 3:34 reminds us that God loves the Son and that he loves us without limit for "God gives the Spirit without limit."

Jesus hinted about a new understanding of worship in his conversation with the Samaritan woman at Jacob's well (4:4-26). As is so often the case, the woman tried to sidetrack Jesus's train of thought by introducing a religious controversy between Jews and Samaritans about the proper location for true worship. Rather than sidetracking him, Jesus used her comment to make his point in a profound way. He said, "Yet a time is coming and has now come when the true worshipers will worship the Father in the Spirit and in truth, for they are the kind of worshipers the Father seeks. God is spirit, and his worshipers must worship in the Spirit and in truth" (v. 23). Jesus introduces us to Trinitarian worship in the new covenant. Our worship is "directed toward the Father, empowered by the presence of [the] Spirit, and grounded in the truth embodied in Jesus."[9]

In John 6, Jesus gave his disciples another hint about the involvement of the Holy Spirit in their spiritual lives (vv. 60-64). Many who followed Jesus at a distance and perhaps did not believe in him or had not committed themselves to remain faithful through hardship found Jesus's teaching hard to accept (v. 60). Jesus's comment in verse 62 implies that those who doubted that Jesus came from heaven would find it even harder to believe that Jesus would soon return to heaven. More importantly, the reference to

---

9. Laura Sweat Holmes and George Lyons, *John 1–12*, New Beacon Bible Commentary (Kansas City: Beacon Hill Press of Kansas City, 2020), 135.

the Holy Spirit in verse 63 should really catch our attention. Here Jesus affirmed that the life-giving power of his words and life come from the Holy Spirit: "They are full of the Spirit and life." Therefore, those who believe in him and his message have the same life-giving Spirit living in them as well. Jesus's teaching about the Holy Spirit here sounds similar to what he said to Nicodemus in John 3.

In John 7, Jesus offered one additional hint about the timing of the Holy Spirit's infilling of believers (vv. 37-39). Jesus spoke at the Feast of Tabernacles, which celebrated the spiritual significance of water and light. Believers recognized Jesus as the embodiment of both Old Testament symbols. With reference to Isaiah 55:1 and 12:3, Jesus invited the spiritually thirsty to find refreshment in him. He said that believing in him would someday give them an ever-flowing river from within. Jesus used this imagery to refer to being filled with the Holy Spirit. John offered an important clue about the timing of this infilling in John 7:39. This incredible promise of the infilling of the Holy Spirit would become a reality in the lives of his disciples after his crucifixion, resurrection, and ascension to the Father.[10]

The Best Is Yet to Come

The work of the Holy Spirit in the life and ministry of Jesus deserves much more attention than this chapter can provide. I hope the frequent biblical references connecting God the Son and God the Holy Spirit in the four gospels will prompt you to do further study. To this point in our study, we have traced the involvement of the Holy Spirit in the plan of salvation for humanity through the Old Testament and the incarnation of Jesus Christ. Most of the detail about the Father's plan to fill believers with the Holy Spirit

---

10. Ibid., 198-99.

comes from the words of Jesus, who knew the Father and the Spirit intimately.

Jesus saved his fuller explanation of the ministry of the Holy Spirit in the lives of believers for his last extended conversation with them on the night of the Last Supper in the upper room. We now turn our attention to that conversation for some of the most incredible revelations about God's plan that Jesus's disciples had ever heard.

Words to Describe the Holy Spirit

1. Leader
2. Guide
3. Empowerer
4. Fulfiller
5. Anointer
6. Life Giving

Questions for Reflection

1. Name all the ways that you can think of that the Holy Spirit worked in the life, ministry, and teaching of Jesus Christ.

2. How did the Holy Spirit work to prepare Jesus for his death, resurrection, and ascension?

3. What do you learn about the Trinity when you read about Jesus's baptism by John the Baptist in the Jordan River?

4. How have mountaintop spiritual experiences been followed by times of trial or testing in your spiritual journey?

5. How did the Holy Spirit assist Jesus during his wilderness temptation experience?

6. What does Jesus teach you from his wilderness experience about resisting temptation?

7. Why do you think the hometown folks in Nazareth found it so hard to accept Jesus as a fulfillment of Isaiah 61:1-2?

8. What does the ministry of both Elijah and Elisha to Gentiles tell you about God's interest in all the peoples of the world?

9. Why is the promise of the Father to give us the Holy Spirit (Luke 11:11-13) so important?

10. In what ways are the involvement of the Holy Spirit in the life of Jesus on earth and the Spirit's involvement in your life similar?

SEVEN

Final Instructions

Do not let your hearts be troubled. You believe in God; believe also in me.

—John 14:1

Every true Christian now "receives the Holy Ghost," as the Paraclete or Comforter promised by our Lord.

—John Wesley[1]

Making the Pieces Fit

My doctoral dissertation was a religious history of the Amana people located in East Central Iowa. These German residents immigrated to the United States in 1843 to gain religious freedom to worship as radical German Pietists. They established the longest lasting and most successful religious commune in American history. Their faith interested me because they came from a religious tradition that heavily influenced John and Charles Wesley.

The historians of the Amana Colonies kept detailed records of the spiritual, social, and business interactions of the community for more than one hundred years. So I researched a wealth of primary resources in analyzing their faith and the way it influenced their lifestyle. After more than two years of reading and writing about these incred-

---

1. Wesley, "A Farther Appeal to Men of Reason and Religion," part 1, in *Works of John Wesley*, 8:104.

ible people, I hit a wall. Something happened within the community in 1932 that caused them to dissolve the religious commune and move to a for-profit business model. What happened? Other scholars had surmised that as their faith waned, their commitment to the commune failed. I didn't agree with that theory but did not have an acceptable alternative.

Then the Lord gave me a great idea. I decided to personally interview every member of the community who lived through the 1932 transition. I sat in every cottage and listened to those dear saints tell the story from their perspective. By the conclusion of the exercise, colony members gave me a fuller picture. I now had an acceptable alternative to the loss-of-faith theory. I concluded that the shift to a for-profit business model did not occur due to a lack of faith in God or the community. It happened because the stock market crash of 1929 threw the entire nation into a depression that dried up the markets for the food, meat, woolen products, and furniture the Amana Colonies sold to the general public. They struggled for more than two years following the crash of the stock market to maintain a positive cash flow. However, the depression finally forced them into a different business model. By the way, the Amana people survived the depression and continue to thrive today, nearly two hundred years after their arrival in the United States. My wife and I visit them nearly every year.

This story illustrates a significant transition in our study of the Holy Spirit. To this point, we have reviewed the work of the Spirit in creation and providence, in assigning specific tasks to individuals, in speaking through the prophets about the coming Messiah, and in preparing the way for the Messiah's arrival. Jesus Christ demonstrated the power of the Spirit at work in his preaching and teaching ministry. Everything we have said so far has contributed to our understanding of God's self-revelation and plan of salvation for humanity. Yet each prophecy and reference to the Spirit made by Jesus gives us another puzzle piece to add to our collection.

I feel at this point the way I felt when I hit a wall in my dissertation on the Amana Colonies. What are we missing? How do we put the puzzle pieces together to visualize a picture of the Holy Spirit at work in our lives today? I think the answer is twofold. First, we need to sit at the feet of Jesus and listen carefully to his last extended conversation with his disciples. Here he carefully explained the work the Holy Spirit would do following his return to the Father. The insights Jesus shared with his disciples in John 14–16 will do for us what my interviews with Amana Colony residents did for my dissertation study. That will be the focus of this chapter. Second, we need to look at the work of the Holy Spirit in the book of Acts and the church. We will focus on that in the following chapter.

Final Conversation

Jesus had just shared the Last Supper together with his disciples. As soon as Judas left to betray Jesus, the mood in the room changed. Jesus opened his heart to prepare his friends for the events to come later that evening as well as in the days ahead. Ironic, don't you think? In just a few hours, Jesus would be arrested, tried, found guilty, beaten, mocked, ridiculed, hung on a criminal's cross, and die. Yet in that hour his love for his disciples focused his attention on them and their needs, not his.

Jesus started by urging his disciples not to be troubled by what lay ahead and then challenged them to trust him and his Father (John 14:1-14). In a profound way he brought together many Old Testament promises and prophecies of the new covenant as he explained to them, and us, exactly how God was about to "put my law in their minds and write it on their hearts" (Jer. 31:33) as he put his Spirit in

The Holy Spirit would come into the hearts of believers only after the Father gave his Son for the sins of the world.

them to move them to follow him and live in personal relationship with him (Ezek. 36:25-28). The disciples had recited these promises and prophecies throughout their lives. Now they were about to see them come to life in their own hearts.

The disciples would soon receive God's gift promised throughout the ages. Most gifts have at least four characteristics. First, they express love and appreciation from one person to another. Second, they come without cost and are not earned. Third, they are a remembrance to be treasured and kept. Fourth, a refusal to accept the gift dishonors the giver.[2] The promised Holy Spirit had all four of those characteristics. He would come to Jesus's disciples as an expression of God's incredible love for them. Though this gift would cost them nothing more than their allegiance and commitment to God, the Holy Spirit would come into the hearts of believers only after the Father gave his Son for the sins of the world. The disciples would soon treasure the presence of the Holy Spirit in their lives as a continuing expression of God's faithfulness to his covenant with humanity and his love for them. The disciples wanted everything God planned for them. So they would follow Jesus's instructions carefully to receive this incredible gift of God.

The insights Jesus offered his disciples about the infilling of the Holy Spirit in John 14–16 give us more information about the Spirit than any other place in the entire Bible. It is like an ever-flowing fountain of new insights into this incredible gift of God. I say that to confess that the consideration given to Jesus's words in this chapter do little more than point you in a direction so the Spirit can teach you about himself as you read this Scripture again and again.

---

2. Carter, *Person and Ministry*, 130.

A Unique Name

Jesus caught his disciples' attention, and ours, when he called this gift of God by a unique name (John 14:16). The authors of the Synoptic Gospels and John to this point in his Gospel have used the ancient Greek word *pneuma* for the Holy Spirit. The word corresponds to the Old Testament Hebrew word *ruach*. We encounter this word often when discussing Old Testament promises and prophecies about the coming of the Holy Spirit. The word translates into English as "breath," "wind," "spirit," or "soul." Instead of saying *pneuma* as the disciples had come to expect, Jesus said *paraklētos*. As often happens when translating a word from one language to another, this ancient Greek word has no English equivalent. The best we can do is offer a variety of English words that approximate the meaning and hope that together these possibilities communicate Jesus's meaning. Possible translations for *paraklētos* include "advocate," "comforter," "defender," "consoler," "counselor," "patron," "mediator," "friend," "helper," "strength giver," "intermediary," "legal aide," "revealer," and "intercessor."

I tend to move back and forth in my thinking between several of these possible translations depending on the context in which the Holy Spirit is working in my life. I think of him as my comforter in times of sorrow or loss. He is my mediator, interceding with the Father on my behalf with my burdened prayer requests. I think of him as my friend during our daily conversations. I visualize him as my advocate when I need someone to speak for me and represent me in situations beyond my control. The Holy Spirit does all of this and much more as he stands with us through the ups and downs of life.

Notice in verse 16 that Jesus referred to the Holy Spirit as "another advocate." This leads us to believe that he considered himself to be the disciples' first advocate. Now that he was physically leaving them in this world, Jesus prepared them

As the third member of the Trinity, God the Holy Spirit is the essence of truth, since he defines truth by his very nature.

for the one who would be in them until the day they reunited with Jesus in their heavenly home (14:1-4). That is clear from Jesus's use of the word "forever" (v. 16). "Unlike Jesus, the Paraclete remains with the believers forever . . . to provide a permanent presence of God with the community."[3]

Jesus referred to the Paraclete as the "Spirit of truth" (14:17; 15:26; 16:13). You have, no doubt, heard people say during times of confusion, "I just wish we could get to the truth." The Spirit guarantees us all the truth we need to worship God correctly, know Jesus as our personal Savior, and live in daily relationship with him. He tells us the truth about God plainly and simply. As the third member of the Trinity, God the Holy Spirit is the essence of truth, since he defines truth by his very nature. Those who live according to the standards and values of the world cannot know God in this way or experience the infilling of the Spirit. The world's definition of truth relies on scientific theory and popular public opinion. Many in society today believe they have the power to define truth; they say truth is whatever they decide it to be.

Jesus is speaking here not about scientific theory or popular public opinion. Rather, he reminds us that the truth that sets us free comes from God, is spiritual, and is known through relationship with him. Remember in chapter 4 of this book that we discussed Old Testament prophecies promising a day when the Holy Spirit of God would live in the hearts of believers. Jesus reminds his disciples of this again by saying the Spirit of Truth would live in them (14:17).

Promised Return

Jesus attempted to calm his disciples' fear of the unknown triggered by this conversation. Earlier he said, "Do not let your hearts be troubled" (John 14:1). He followed

---

3. Robert Kysar, quoted in Lyons and Daniels, *John 13–21*, 82.

this in verse 18 with, "I will not leave you as orphans; I will come to you." Scholars debate his meaning. I think this promise has at least three fulfillments: Jesus's post-resurrection appearances to his disciples; the continuing, abiding presence of the Holy Spirit following Pentecost; and the second coming of Christ.

Those who live by the world's values and standards will not "see" Jesus as he promised to reveal himself to his disciples, because seeing Jesus requires eyes of faith. Hebrews 11 reminds us that faith is an essential element of seeing, knowing, and believing in God's work in our world. Another essential element is obedience. "Whoever has my commands and keeps them is the one who loves me" (John 14:21). Jesus instructed his disciples to love one another earlier in this conversation (13:34-35). Jesus referred to this as "a new command" (v. 34). Why did he call it new, since the Old Testament commanded us to love one another centuries ago (Lev. 19:18)? It's likely that Jesus calls it new because he commands us to love as he loves—that is, selflessly, humbly, and to the point of death (Phil. 2:5-11).

Covenant Invitation

We often refer to the mystery surrounding the interaction of Father, Son, and Holy Spirit as Trinity. True, we will never fully understand how the members of the Trinity relate to one another. We are creatures of God's handiwork. How could we possibly know all that can be known about our creator? However, Jesus invites his disciples, and us, to participate in the love relationship shared among members of the Trinity.

The language of John 14:20 draws our attention to the covenants God made with Abraham and Moses. The Israelites throughout the Old Testament worshipped and related to God by keeping the commands of those covenants. Over time, those commands multiplied from ten to over six hun-

The Paraclete, Holy Spirit, lives in us and makes possible the love relationship we have with the Father and Son. In so doing, he re-creates the love relationship with God that Adam and Eve lost in the fall!

dred. Experts of the law taught exact instructions selected with tweezers to parse the law down to minute details. God's meaning and purpose in that covenant got lost in translation. Now Jesus tells his disciples about a new covenant between God and his followers. This new covenant does not require obedience to a long list of laws. Rather, it invites us to share in the love relationship among members of the Trinity.

The love Jesus commands his disciples to demonstrate to one another and the world does not come from their own natural abilities but from the heart of God. He shares his love with us; we, in turn, share that love with one another. "I [Jesus] am in my Father, and you are in me, and I am in you" (v. 20). The Paraclete, Holy Spirit, lives in us and makes possible the love relationship we have with the Father and Son. In so doing, he re-creates the love relationship with God that Adam and Eve lost in the fall! Incredibly, this new covenant will be everything the Old Testament promises and prophecies claimed it would be. John 15 is devoted to the vital relationship between the Father, Son, and us.

Personal Tutor

Much of what Jesus told his disciples made no sense to them prior to Jesus's resurrection. Put yourself in the sandals of his disciples. How could they possibly process the large volume of material Jesus shared with them during his three-year teaching and preaching ministry? Even the evening of final instructions recorded in John's Gospel puzzled them. Jesus knew they felt overwhelmed and confused. So he eased their minds when he said, "All this I have spoken while still with you. But the Advocate, the Holy Spirit, whom the Father will send in my name, will teach you all things and will remind you of everything I have said to you" (John 14:25-26).

The same Holy Spirit who gave Old Testament spiritual leaders the promises and prophecies about the coming Messiah will teach and remind Jesus's disciples of the incredible spiritual truths Jesus taught during his incarnation. The mysteries of God's plan of salvation for humanity cannot be unlocked by human intelligence alone. Only the instruction of God's Spirit can reveal these mysteries to believers. Jesus reminded his disciples many times of truths he had taught previously. Now the Holy Spirit would carry on the task of reminding us of spiritual truths we so easily forget. We must remember,

> The indwelling spirit quickens minds, aids memories, directs the mind to penetrating insights of truth, animates the expression of truth, and in many other ways serves the minds of believers in relation to truth. But perhaps the greatest practical value of the spirit to the believer in relation to the truth is his illumination of the mind to comprehend the message of the revelation given in the Bible.[4]

The Holy Spirit did not teach and remind Jesus's disciples of all he said to them as an intellectual exercise for their academic achievement. Jesus planned for the disciples to carry on his mission and ministry to the world (vv. 12-14). But they could never accomplish the work of Jesus in their own strength and ability. Hence, the Spirit continued the teaching ministry of Jesus with his disciples to prepare them to be witnesses to the world about Jesus and his gospel message.

The teaching ministry of the Holy Spirit within the hearts of Jesus's disciples reminds us again of the symbiotic relationship between members of the Trinity. Jesus did not intend to imply any subordinate relationship of the Spirit to the Son when he said the Spirit would remind Jesus's disci-

---

4. Carter, *Person and Ministry*, 129.

ples of Jesus's preaching and teaching. He intended, rather, to show us that Jesus taught us everything we need to know to find forgiveness for our sins, a relationship with God, and ways to live in the world that please God. No new spiritual revelation exists beyond the revelation of the living Word, Jesus Christ. Therefore, the teaching ministry of the Holy Spirit always points us back to Jesus. That is why Jesus said, "When the Advocate comes, whom I will send to you from the Father—the Spirit of truth who goes out from the Father—he will testify about me" (John 15:26). "The Spirit's role was not to guide the church 'into further new truth, but into the truth concerning that which was concretely and concisely set forth by the Son of God.'"[5]

Jesus did not imply separate roles between members of the Trinity. Some scholars have used John 15:26 to say the Holy Spirit came to us from the Father alone; others say he came from the Father and the Son.[6] Jesus is not calling our attention to the internal functions of the various members of the Trinity. Rather, he is telling us that the Father and Son took the next step in the redemption of humanity by sending the Holy Spirit to take the mission of God to the next level—that is, to what we know today as the church age. We enjoy the privilege of living in the age of the church. The Holy Spirit works through the community of believers to continue God's mission to the world through us.

Jesus reaffirmed the work of the Holy Spirit when he said, "He will glorify me because it is from me that he will receive what he will make known to you. All that belongs to the Father is mine. That is why I said the Spirit will receive

---

5. Edward W. Klink III, quoted in Lyons and Daniels, *John 13–21*, 110.
6. This disagreement is known as the *filioque* debate. *Filioque* means "and from the Son." The Eastern church took the position that the Holy Spirit proceeded from the Father alone; the Western church said the Holy Spirit came from the Father and the Son. The Eastern and Western churches divided in AD 1054 with the *filioque* debate at the center of their disagreements.

from me what he will make known to you" (16:14-15). The Holy Spirit always seeks to glorify Jesus Christ; that must be our primary task in life as well. "To glorify Jesus is to praise him as the definitive Revealer of God. . . . It is to recognize him as God incarnate and to honor him as the divine Revealer and Redeemer."[7]

A Hard Truth

Jesus's disciples were saddened and grieved by his final instructions (John 16:6). They could not grasp this hard truth that Jesus had to leave them to make way for the Holy Spirit to infill them. "But very truly I tell you, it is for your good that I am going away. Unless I go away, the Advocate will not come to you; but if I go, I will send him to you" (v. 7). As comforting as Jesus intended those words to be, his disciples could not possibly grasp all that the Father, Son, and Holy Spirit had in store for them.

Three Tasks

Our vantage point in salvation history gives us the privilege of knowing what the Holy Spirit has been doing in the church age. Jesus said, "When he [the Holy Spirit] comes, he will prove the world to be in the wrong about sin and righteousness and judgment: about sin, because people do not believe in me; about righteousness, because I am going to the Father, where you can see me no longer; and about judgment, because the prince of this world now stands condemned" (John 16:8-11). So, Jesus highlighted three tasks the Holy Spirit undertakes as he strives with our hearts.

First, he impresses on us that our understanding of sin is wrong if we think it is only someone else's problem;

---

7. Lyons and Daniels, *John 13–21*, 111.

we, too, are sinners in need of a Savior. Jesus is the only Savior for humanity. The very essence of sin is the refusal to believe in Jesus and worship him as Lord.

Second, he lifts the standard of righteousness to the life of Jesus. He defines righteousness itself and illustrates it in word and deed. He points out the error of self-righteousness that we often hide behind and calls us to the righteousness that only Jesus offers.

Third, he reminds everyone that judgment day is coming whether sinners choose to believe it or not. Popular opinion polls have written the idea of judgment out of common belief and the doctrinal statements of many churches. But the Holy Spirit has the final word. Satan and his followers have already been condemned. We will all someday stand before the judgment court of God and give an account of our lives.

Peace

Jesus concluded his final conversation with his disciples in John 16 the way he began it in John 14, with words of comfort. He began by saying, "Do not let your hearts be troubled" (v. 1); he ended with, "I have told you these things, so that in me you may have peace. In this world you will have trouble. But take heart! I have overcome the world" (16:33). Notice that Jesus did not say he would insulate his disciples from all trouble. Quite the contrary; following Jesus would set them up for certain opposition from the world and all who oppose Jesus (15:18-25). The peace Jesus promised would result from keeping their hearts and minds focused on Jesus himself. He would be their peace in the midst of troubling circumstances and outright persecution.

Keeping our hearts and minds focused on Jesus involves more than remembering his earthly teaching and preaching. We don't just look through the recollections of our memory. Rather, the abiding Holy Spirit, the promise of the Father, brings to us the presence of our living Lord. His presence overshadows us with peace just as his presence calmed the storm on the Sea of Galilee (Matt. 8:23-27).

Beginning and Ending

Most of this chapter has focused on Jesus's final instructions to his disciples in John 14–16. We learn more about the person and work of the Holy Spirit in these chapters than in any other chapter of the Bible. The entire conversation of Jesus flows from a proper understanding of the Trinity, especially as God establishes a new covenant with humanity through the incarnation of Christ. We now see a much bigger picture of God's plan of salvation for us. Jesus wanted his disciples to begin to grasp the notion that the promised Holy Spirit is God just as the Father and Son are God.

Matthew's Gospel bookends the earthly ministry of Jesus with clear references to the Trinity. We see the earthly ministry of Jesus begin at his baptism. Father, Son, and Holy Spirit participate in that event (Matt. 3:13-17). The earthly ministry of Jesus ended with a reference to the Trinity as well. Matthew concluded his Gospel with these words: "Then Jesus came to them and said, 'All authority in heaven and on earth has been given to me. Therefore go and make disciples of all nations, baptizing them in the name of the Father and of the Son and of the Holy Spirit, and teaching them to obey everything I have commanded you. And surely I am with you always, to the very end of the age'" (28:18-20).

Notice two observations in what Jesus said. First, he declared that he broke the grip of Satan on the hearts and lives of people since the fall. No longer would people have to feel powerless in sin's grip. Jesus triumphed over Satan in the wilderness temptations as well as in his death and resurrection. "All authority in heaven and on earth" has now been given to him. Jesus is Lord of all humanity. Next, he reminded his disciples that they are to "make disciples of all nations." As they baptize new believers into the faith, they are to use the Trinitarian formula, in the name of the Father, of the Son, and of the Holy Spirit. The closing words of Matthew's Gospel remind us that we are never alone. Through the presence and power of the Holy Spirit, Jesus is with us to the "end of the age"!

Words to Describe the Holy Spirit

1. Advocate
2. Comforter
3. Defender
4. Intercessor

Questions for Reflection

1. What thoughts would have been going through your head if you had been with the disciples in the upper room when Jesus had his last extended conversation with them (John 14–16)?

2. What questions would you have had for Jesus if you had been in the upper room for that last extended conversation?

3. How is it possible that the Holy Spirit continues to teach us new lessons about himself and Jesus every time we read John 14–16?

4. Which translations of the word *paraklētos* have the most meaning in your life right now? Why do you think this is true?

5. In what ways was Jesus an advocate for his disciples during his earthly ministry?

6. What does the title "Spirit of Truth" tell you about the ministry of the Holy Spirit?

7. Why do you think public opinion and individual belief carry so much authority in defining truth in today's society?

8. What are the dangers in allowing public opinion and individual belief to carry authority in defining truth?

9. How is the new covenant God entered into with humanity better than the old one?

10. How does the peace of God manifest itself in your life?

EIGHT: Radical Transformation

May God himself, the God of peace, sanctify you through and through. May your whole spirit, soul and body be kept blameless at the coming of our Lord Jesus Christ.
—1 Thessalonians 5:23

Both inward and outward holiness are consequent on this faith, and are the ordinary, stated condition of final justification. . . . I not only allow, but vehemently contend, that none shall ever enter into glory who is not holy on earth, as well in heart, as "in all manner of conversation."
—John Wesley[1]

Learning to Wait

I clearly remember my first experience in learning to wait. My elementary school hero visited our house every Saturday morning by television. The Lone Ranger rode his faithful horse Silver across the plains of West Texas saving the residents from the robbers and bad guys who meant them harm. The back of my favorite breakfast cereal box invited me to join the Lone Ranger's club as a deputy marshal for free. All I had to do was collect ten box tops from my breakfast cereal and mail them in. I ate cereal like crazy to hurry and empty ten boxes; I enlisted the help of my sister and two brothers in eating as much cereal as they could each morning.

---

1. Wesley, "Farther Appeal to Men," part 1, in *Works of John Wesley*, 8:56.

I soon collected all ten box tops and dropped them in the mail. Then I waited. I hoped the Lone Ranger needed my assistance immediately so he would hurry and get me enrolled in his club. I watched for the postal carrier and ran to the mailbox every day as I waited for my special package. Then it finally arrived. I couldn't open the box fast enough. It contained a red neckerchief, a metal deputy badge, and a certificate suitable for framing that identified me as a deputy marshal. I wore that badge and neck scarf every Saturday as I watched my hero save the Wild West.

Wait for the Promise

The disciples of Jesus also learned to wait as they followed Jesus through his last days with them. They rode an emotional roller coaster from the last extended conversation recorded in John 14–16 to his ascension to the Father recorded in Luke 24:50-53 and Acts 1:1-11. Luke added additional detail in his Acts account that he did not include in his Gospel account. Luke named the Holy Spirit three times in the first chapter of Acts: verses 2, 5, and 16. He credited the Holy Spirit with empowering Jesus as he gave final instructions to his disciples and inspiring David with a prophecy about Judas Iscariot. Jesus's words in 1:4-5 catch our attention because they command the disciples to wait in Jerusalem until they are baptized with the Holy Spirit. The few days the disciples waited seem short in comparison to the centuries the Israelites had waited for God to fulfill the promises made through the prophets about the coming age of the Spirit.

Jesus reminded his disciples of John the Baptist's testimony about Jesus. John said, "I baptize you with water for repentance. But after me comes one who is more powerful than I, whose sandals I am not worthy to carry. He will baptize you with the Holy Spirit and fire" (Matt. 3:11). Then Jesus said to his disciples just prior to his ascension back to the Father, "For John baptized with water, but in a few days you will be baptized with the Holy Spirit" (Acts 1:5). The disciples shared the preconceived ideas that had circulated among the Israelites for centuries. They believed the coming of God's Spirit signaled the return of the golden age of King David's reign (Isa. 32:14-20). They assumed Jesus was about to drive the Roman Empire from the land of Israel and reestablish independence to their nation. They saw the kingdom of God coming in great glory, since even the surrounding Gentile nations would convert to Israel's God (2:2-4).[2]

Jesus quickly turned the attention of his disciples back to his instructions about the Holy Spirit as he filled their hearts with a message of promise and hope: "But you will receive power when the Holy Spirit comes on you; and you will be my witnesses in Jerusalem, and in all Judea and Samaria, and to the ends of the earth" (Acts 1:8). So the purpose of the Holy Spirit's empowerment would be to enable the disciples to witness about the life, ministry, death, and resurrection of Jesus to all the peoples of the earth. That global inclusion echoed Jesus's words to Nicodemus: "For God so loved the world that he gave his one and only Son, that whoever believes in him shall not perish but have eternal life. For God did not send his Son into the world to condemn the world, but to save the world through him" (John 3:16-17).

Jesus ascended back to his Father, and his disciples returned to Jerusalem to wait. They gathered in the upper room where they had celebrated the Last Supper with Jesus forty days earlier, and they joined together in prayer. This proved to be a unifying experience for Jesus's disciples. They had experienced several trying times over the past

---

2. Richard P. Thompson, *Acts*, New Beacon Bible Commentary (Kansas City: Beacon Hill Press of Kansas City, 2015), 59-60.

several weeks. Now with Jesus absent from the group, they needed a new catalyst to draw them back together. They prayed through each day and into the evening for more than a week. They didn't know how long they would be together like this or exactly what to expect. Jesus seemed to indicate that when his promise reached its fulfillment among them, they would have no doubt. So they waited for something dramatic to happen.

The Promise Fulfilled

Dramatic doesn't begin to describe what took place in that upper room. On the tenth day of their prayer meeting, the heavens broke open and the promised Holy Spirit filled them to the depth of their being (Acts 2:1-4). It happened on the day of Pentecost. Just as God gave marvelous signs when he instituted a new contract with Moses, he gave the disciples marvelous signs with their new contract.

When God gave Moses the Ten Commandments, the Hebrew nation put on clean clothes, prepared their hearts, and waited. On the third day of their wait, a dark cloud covered Mount Sinai. Out of the cloud came bright lightning, loud thunder, and a very loud trumpet blast. Smoke billowed up from the mountain as fire descended from heaven. The mountain shook as if being ripped apart by an earthquake (Exod. 19:14-19). All of these sights and sounds signaled the presence and power of God.

The sights and sounds of Pentecost also signaled the presence and power of God. A great wind blew through their prayer meeting. It symbolized the breath of God, first blowing over everything on the days of creation and then bending down and blowing life into the nostrils of the first human being. Flames of fire descended on each person at the prayer meeting. These flames symbolized purity of heart. They all began proclaiming the gospel message in languages that they had never learned. They went to the streets and told the thousands of Jerusalem visitors about Jesus Christ. This symbolized the need to take the gospel message to the ends of the earth. Remember, these were the same people who hid from the religious and civil authorities behind locked doors just a few days before. Now in the power of the Holy Spirit, they were out in public, telling everyone about Jesus Christ.[3]

Jesus had certainly fulfilled his promise beyond their wildest imaginations. The Holy Spirit came upon them in ways they could never doubt. They literally talked about that day for the rest of their lives. We know this because when a council meeting of the Christian church convened twenty years later, Peter was still rehearsing what the Holy Spirit did in their hearts on the day of Pentecost and in the hearts of Gentiles who were later filled with the Holy Spirit (Acts 15:1-21). By that time the church had spread far beyond the boundaries of Jerusalem, Israel, and the Middle East. It gained strength in established congregations all over the Roman Empire and continued unrestrained growth and expansion.

The Christian church no longer consisted of Jews alone, as in the beginning. Countless Gentiles also called themselves Christians as well. Peter, in speaking to the Jerusalem Council, added a new thought to what happened when the Holy Spirit filled them. To the idea of being filled with power from God (1:8), Peter added that the Holy Spirit also "purified their hearts by faith" (15:9).

Prophecies Fulfilled

The baptism with the Holy Spirit brought to reality the prophecies we studied in Jeremiah 31:31-33 and Ezekiel 36:23, 25-27 (see ch. 4 of this book). Peter recognized Joel's

---

3. Other references to being filled with the Spirit include Acts 4:8, 31; 13:9, 52; 19:6; Eph. 5:18.

vision realized at Pentecost. Thus he quoted Joel 2:28-29 in his Pentecost sermon. God also fulfilled another Old Testament prophecy we have not studied yet. Malachi 3:1-3 says,

"I will send my messenger, who will prepare the way before me. Then suddenly the Lord you are seeking will come to his temple; the messenger of the covenant, whom you desire, will come," says the Lord Almighty.

But who can endure the day of his coming? Who can stand when he appears? For he will be like a refiner's fire or a launderer's soap. He will sit as a refiner and purifier of silver; he will purify the Levites and refine them like gold and silver. Then the Lord will have men who will bring offerings in righteousness.

We believe the messenger in verse 1 refers to John the Baptist preparing the way for the ministry of Jesus Christ. The Lord's coming, then, refers to the incarnation of Christ, who came and lived among us (John 1:14). The two images in Malachi 3:2, "refiner's fire" and "launderer's soap," refer to word pictures with which people in Bible days were familiar. Metalworkers used fire to refine or purify metal ore of all impurities. Launderer's soap, such as alkali powder, cleaned clothes from dirt and stains. Both images refer to God's judgment, not as a punishment, but as methods of purifying his people so they can serve him in holiness and righteousness. "Both people and things used in the tabernacle and temple must be cleansed of anything that is unacceptable to God. This is an essential part of the process that prepares them to be set apart (made holy) for their task."[4]

Malachi's prophecy came true on the day of Pentecost. When the Holy Spirit entered the hearts of waiting believers, he both cleansed them from inbred sin and empowered

---

4. Laurie J. Braaten and Jim Edlin, *Nahum–Malachi*, New Beacon Bible Commentary (Kansas City: Beacon Hill Press of Kansas City, 2019), 395-96.

their witness for God. This brought immediate growth in the church. This new community of faith reminds us of another hope the Father had in the beginning. He always wanted followers who would separate themselves from other identities so they could be his special possession.

God shared his hope with Moses that the nation of Israel might be his special possession: "For you are a people holy to the Lord your God. The Lord your God has chosen you out of all the peoples on the face of the earth to be his people, his treasured possession" (Deut. 7:6). Think about that phrase "treasured possession." The creator of a thousand galaxies, across a million light years, most highly treasures his family members! Later in the book, God shared his vision again: "For you are a people holy to the Lord your God. Out of all the peoples on the face of the earth, the Lord has chosen you to be his treasured possession" (14:2).

The Old Testament reveals that the nation of Israel never fulfilled God's dreams for them. Once the church began to take shape following the miraculous events of Pentecost, God's desire for a special people resurfaced. Peter saw God's special possession coming through the church: "But you are a chosen people, a royal priesthood, a holy nation, God's special possession, that you may declare the praises of him who called you out of darkness into his wonderful light" (1 Pet. 2:9). Peter's analysis of the Christian church sounds much like God's hopes for a special people described in Deuteronomy 7:6. Peter saw God's dream come to reality at Pentecost. With the infilling of the Holy Spirit, a new relationship with believers brought the possibility of God having his treasured possession.

As mentioned at the beginning of the last chapter, we learn about the Holy Spirit in two primary ways. Jesus gave us a deeper level of understanding of the Spirit in his last extended conversation with his disciples recorded in

The book of Acts illustrates the work of the Holy Spirit in the early church. The transformation that took place in that community of faith resulted from the transformation that took place in the hearts and lives of individuals who made up that community.

John 14–16. The other picture of the Holy Spirit at work in our world comes from the events of Pentecost and the remainder of the book of Acts. Acts, often referred to as the Acts of the Apostles, details rather the acts of the Holy Spirit working through believers in the early church. Every chapter of Acts tells a new story of the Holy Spirit's work in the community of faith and the lives of individuals in that community (13:2, 4; 15:28; 16:6-7; 20:28).

Several years ago our pastor preached a sermon series that he called Acts 29. The book of Acts, as you know, concluded with chapter 28. Our pastor highlighted in his sermon series how the Holy Spirit continued to write the history of the church through the work done in our congregation. That sermon series could be preached in churches around the world where the Holy Spirit continues to bless and empower believers to preach the gospel of Jesus Christ and live holy lives as witnesses to his transforming power.

Trees and the Forest

A forest consists of individual trees. When we speak about what happens in a forest, such as rain that falls on it or fire that attacks it, we are thinking about what happens to individual trees within that forest. The same is true for God's church. God worked with the entire Hebrew nation throughout the Old Testament, but he also had relationships with individuals within that community of faith. The book of Acts illustrates the work of the Holy Spirit in the early church. The transformation that took place in that community of faith resulted from the transformation that took place in the hearts and lives of individuals who made up that community. We must always consider the work the Holy Spirit does both in the corporate body and in individuals.

Paul understood that dynamic as he wrote Romans 5:12–8:39. He understood that God's work in the community of faith in both the Old and New Testaments occurred as he worked with individuals within those communities. We want to now take a closer look at the work of the Holy Spirit in transforming believers into Christlike disciples through the power of the gospel of Jesus Christ.

A Big Picture Perspective

Paul begins in Romans 5:12 by reviewing our problem with the sin nature—that twist in our thinking toward self-preference. Adam and Eve's sinful choice threw all humanity out of balance with God and themselves (vv. 12-14). Christ came as a second Adam, exposed himself to the same temptations, and obeyed God. He did what Adam and Eve did not do. He then went to the cross for our salvation. Thus Christ made possible an undoing of Adam and Eve's damage. That is what led Paul to say, "For just as through the disobedience of the one man the many were made sinners, so also through the obedience of the one man the many will be made righteous" (v. 19). The grace and gift of God in Christ Jesus destroys sin's dominion over us (vv. 20-21).

Once sin's power over us is broken, we are freed to live a new kind of life. How? By identifying with Christ in his crucifixion, our old life of sin dies. The act of baptism symbolizes this death as we are buried in a water grave and raised up to new spiritual life. In this way our old sinful self, unregenerate and away from God, is destroyed. It no longer has power over us. The resurrection life of Jesus Christ working through us replaces it (6:1-10). The individual does not die, but self-sovereignty dies.

With this background of Adam's failure and Christ's success clearly in view, Paul moves on in Romans 6 to a wonderful picture of God's efforts at fulfilling his hopes and dreams in us. Since Christ, by his death on the cross, undid the garden damage, then spiritually speaking, we're back to God's original plan. Paul's discussion throughout Romans 6 weaves its way back and forth between what God does for us and what he expects us to do in response to his actions.

First, Paul says, "Count yourselves dead to sin but alive to God in Christ Jesus" (v. 11). That means we are to live as if God's new life really is at work in us. Why? Because it is. Do we believe something that is not true? No, we believe in the power of God to do as he promised and transform us.

Next, Paul says "not [to] let sin reign in your mortal body so that you obey its evil desires" (v. 12). Christ has broken the power of that reign through his death on the cross. We identify ourselves with his death. God creates the possibility; we respond by living the reality. Since we once chose to sin, we can now choose not to sin. God doesn't remove sin's allure; he breaks the power of sin's desire within us. It's a matter of living with a made-up mind.

Further, "Do not offer any part of yourself to sin as an instrument of wickedness, but rather offer yourselves to God as those who have been brought from death to life; and offer every part of yourself to him as an instrument of righteousness" (v. 13). We leave the old sinful lifestyle behind. We replace that old lifestyle with full devotion to God.

God's grace replaces our bondage to the law. This free grace does not mean we are free to go on sinning. Never! Paul says grace does not offer freedom to sin; it offers freedom from sin. We choose the master we wish to serve. Our old lives brought control by bondage to sin's habits and addictions. Our new master, then, is Christ; our new slavery is righteousness (vv. 14-18). Where does this new contract with God lead? Paul gives the answer in Romans 6:19. It is "righteousness leading to holiness." That's where Paul's argument has been building all along—God's plan leads to our holiness. He continues in verse 22 to say, "The benefit you reap leads to holiness, and the result is eternal life."

Eternal life begins the moment we accept Christ as Savior. It continues to surge through our veins both here on earth and in the timelessness of heaven. All along the way, on this side of heaven's door, we grow in our relationship with God. That growth takes place on the road of holiness.

Do Not Conform

Paul's discussions in Romans 6:11-14 talk about counting ourselves dead to sin but alive to God; he also urges us not to offer the parts of our body to sin. Paul adds another symbol to this thought in Romans 12:1-2. It's his discussion of a living sacrifice. He says, "Therefore, I urge you, brothers and sisters, in view of God's mercy, to offer your bodies as a living sacrifice, holy and pleasing to God—this is your true and proper worship. Do not conform to the pattern of this world, but be transformed by the renewing of your mind. Then you will be able to test and approve what God's will is—his good, pleasing and perfect will."

In consecration we lay ourselves on God's altar just as people in the Old Testament laid sacrifices on the altars of the tabernacle and temple. Gifts brought to the altar in the Old Testament had to be spotless and without blemish. We're neither, but we do have the Holy Spirit living with us, so he makes our consecration to the Father possible. We offer back to him the new life he gives us.

Paul says we present ourselves to God. When he says we offer our bodies, he means we offer every part of our being—body, soul, mind, and strength—to God. Giving God all of the keys to all of the rooms of our heart illustrates this effort. We give him everything of which we are aware and everything that remains in the shadows of the future.

Let us now explore Paul's notion of not conforming to the pattern of this world. Paul is not speaking of the world of nature, with earth, sea, and sky. He is talking about the system of thought that puts the self first and centers the universe around personal motivations. It manifests itself in self-will, self-love, self-trust, and self-exaltation. It seeks

The resurrection power of Jesus Christ flowing through our beings reorients our thinking, our value system, our priorities, our motivations, and our desires. It accomplishes nothing short of a complete renovation of our personal system of thinking and living.

pleasure, power, and position. It places personal needs over the needs of others.

What is the result of this pattern of thinking and living? It damages and destroys relationships with family and friends. It short-circuits concern for others. It ultimately results in loneliness and lack of fulfillment. It leaves a wake of evil and corruption. Satan told Eve, "You will not die" (see Gen. 3:4). He lied. This pattern of thinking always leads to death.

But Be Transformed

When we offer ourselves to God and reject Satan's worldly ways, we save ourselves from heartache and grief. Further, we become candidates for God to transform us from the inside out. That is, he transforms our minds, and transformed minds result in transformed lifestyles. These new lifestyles honor God by seeking to do his will.

The concept of transformation that Paul uses in Romans 12:1-2 suggests what happens when a caterpillar crawling in the dirt changes into a butterfly and takes wing for the sky. The Father transforms us with the same power source he used to raise Jesus from the dead. The resurrection power of Jesus Christ flowing through our beings reorients our thinking, our value system, our priorities, our motivations, and our desires. It accomplishes nothing short of a complete renovation of our personal system of thinking and living. This thorough, radical, universal power surge of resurrection energy through our beings transforms our minds, and this in turn brings about outward lifestyle changes.

Paul continued this thought in 1 Thessalonians: "For God did not call us to be impure, but to live a holy life" (4:7). Then he added, "May God himself, the God of peace, sanctify you through and through. May your whole spirit, soul and body be kept blameless at the coming of our Lord

Jesus Christ. The one who calls you is faithful, and he will do it" (5:23-24). We are responsible for the consecration Paul describes in Romans 12:1-2. Only God can give us the gift of entire sanctification as Paul described in 1 Thessalonians 5:23-24. We receive God's gift by faith just as we received justification by grace through faith (Rom. 1:17). Look again at 1 Thessalonians 5:24: "He will do it."

We obviously are not transformed by our own efforts and personal energy source. It's too miraculous for that. Rather, the Holy Spirit of God transforms us both at a moment in time and in daily living as we allow him to change us. This is what Paul meant in 2 Corinthians 3:18 when he said, "And we, who with unveiled faces contemplate the Lord's glory, are being transformed into his image with ever-increasing glory, which comes from the Lord, who is the Spirit."

God sees infinitely more potential and ability in us than we see in ourselves. One of the miracles of his grace is his miraculous work in taking the little we think we have to offer and multiplying it into a significant accomplishment for his kingdom. He works in us much like Jesus worked with the young boy's lunch during one of his teaching sessions. He used five biscuits and two little fish to cater a banquet for five thousand families (John 6:1-13).

For reasons known only to him, God chooses to build his kingdom through the efforts of one- and two-talent people. Not many mega-talented people serve in the church. Most of us can sing, speak, work with children, mow the grass, or cook a meal for a needy family. Few of us do a variety of things well. God uses everyone nonetheless.

I think I know the reason why. As Paul put it, "For it is by grace you have been saved, through faith—and this is not from yourselves, it is the gift of God—not by works, so that no one can boast" (Eph. 2:8-9). Boasting becomes impossible when we realize God alone accomplishes the good work that flows from our efforts. Only he deserves the praise and glory. So he doesn't ask how many talents we possess; he asks for our faithfulness.

Life in the Spirit

In Romans 7, Paul explained the impossibility of keeping all the laws of the old covenant by our own will and determination. He said this regarding his attempts at keeping the commands of the law: "If someone else thinks they have reasons to put confidence in the flesh, I have more: circumcised on the eighth day, of the people of Israel, of the tribe of Benjamin, a Hebrew of Hebrews; in regard to the law, a Pharisee; as for zeal, persecuting the church; as for righteousness based on the law, faultless" (Phil. 3:4-6). Paul did everything the old covenant required of him, and yet he realized that he failed just as everyone before him had done. "But whatever were gains to me I now consider loss for the sake of Christ" (v. 7). Paul ended his Romans 7 analysis of the failure of the law to make him truly righteous with, "Thanks be to God, who delivers me through Jesus Christ our Lord!" (v. 25).

Then comes the glorious light in Romans 8: "Therefore, there is now no condemnation for those who are in Christ Jesus, because through Christ Jesus the law of the Spirit who gives life has set you free from the law of sin and death" (vv. 1-2). From there Paul contrasted two ways of living. Here is a brief overview of those contrasts.

1. *Two Preferences (8:1, 8-9)*. You may prefer living in Christ Jesus. As a believer, you are in Christ and he is in you. The Spirit of God not only brings the living presence of Christ *to* you but also locates him *in* you. You are united with him in a mystical connection that brings daily communion between your spirit and his Spirit. Your spirit is not absorbed by his so as to nullify your personhood or cancel your

free will. You still make choices and think your own thoughts. The difference centers on your will preferring God's will to such a degree that his will becomes the very spiritual oxygen you breathe.

Conversely, you may prefer living in the flesh. The Bible uses flesh in three main ways: your body, the human point of view, and the carnal nature of humanity that favors the self over God. Paul intends the third way in this passage of Scripture. The flesh represents a world that makes no attempt at pleasing God. It does what it wants, when it wants, and in the manner it wants.

2. *Two Walks (8:1, 4-5, 9)*. You may choose a fleshly walk. This walk stays in step with the music of the world's value system. Self-will, self-seeking, and self-gratification mark the path for this walk. The intention may not be to totally disregard God's ways but rather to prevent his ways from taking preference over your ways.

By contrast, you may choose a spiritual walk. This walk stays in step with God's value system. The will of God marks out the path for this walk. Sometimes this path runs totally counter to what you might choose for yourself. You want God's will so clearly that preferences you might have for yourself seem less important in light of his plans.

3. *Two Laws (8:2)*. The law of the Spirit of life can be yours if you choose it. This law comes not from a rule book or court bench but from the heart of Christ. It guides your thinking, feelings, actions, and attitudes. It's not so much a list of dos and don'ts as it is the boundary lines of the relationship you have with God. That love relationship with God causes you to long for his ways, as taught to us by his Spirit.

If you do not choose the law of the Spirit of life, you, by default, choose the law of death. This law comes from Satan. It tells you that anything goes, that you can do what you please. It's a law that disregards all law. Think what you want to think. Do whatever you want to do. Treat others any way you like. Make yourself happy.

4. *Two Powers (8:3-4)*. You may decide you want to try and live by the power of the Ten Commandments. This law tells us we must follow every regulation precisely to please God. However, it's humanly impossible to keep every regulation precisely. So when you fail or fall short, this law condemns you. It offers no power to succeed or further hope that you can ever meet its demands.

You will find life much more enriching and satisfying if you decide to live in the power of Christ. He became your representative on the cross. In God's eyes, it's just as if you had never sinned. There's a big difference between God forgiving but remembering your sins and God forgiving and forgetting your sins. Christ's power gives you a new heart toward God and a new start with him.

5. *Two Loyalties (8:5)*. Your loyalty may be to the flesh. This loyalty subjects you to the powerful whims of your desires, your addictions, and your passions. You become a slave to every lowly, fallen drive that enters your depraved mind. You obey it, not because you think it is best for you, but because you cannot help yourself. Loyalty to the flesh defies logic or reason.

God gives believers the ability to live with a loyalty to the Spirit. This loyalty draws you to the directives of the Spirit. It aims you toward God's will. Your desires fall subject to God's holy, pure, and good desires for you. Your desires conform to his to the point that, more than anything, you want what he wants. Your pleasure is to do his pleasure.

6. *Two Destinies (8:6-7)*. One of the paths Paul described ultimately leads to death. The end of this path leads to total and final destruction. The final stage of addiction brings total bondage. The final stage of self-seeking brings total selfishness. The final stage of the life of the flesh brings physical, spiritual, psychological, and emotional death.

The other path Paul described leads to life. Ironically, Jesus said to save your life, you lose it (Matt. 16:25). So when you surrender your will, preferences, desires, hopes, dreams, plans, wishes, body, soul, and spirit to God's Spirit, rather than losing your life, you actually gain life to the fullest. Life lived in the Spirit gives you the joys and benefits of eternal life right now.

The Spirit of Christ

Romans 8 offers another important insight about the Holy Spirit. Read verses 9-10. Paul refers to the Holy Spirit as the Spirit of Christ, as did Peter in 1 Peter 1:11. Paul used the designation the Spirit of Jesus Christ in Philippians 1:19. Luke called him the Spirit of Jesus in Acts 16:6-7. We have observed many times throughout this book that all members of the Trinity play roles in the salvation plan for humanity. These references to the Holy Spirit as the Spirit of Christ remind us that Jesus is actively involved in our Christian walk on a daily basis. Through the transforming work of the Holy Spirit we are being transformed into the image of Christ (2 Cor. 3:18).

Words to Describe the Holy Spirit

1. Sanctifier
2. Transformer
3. Spirit of Christ

Questions for Reflection

1. Think of a time in your life when you had to learn a lesson about patience through waiting. With that experience in mind, what thoughts and anxieties might have been running through the disciples' minds as they followed Jesus's instructions to wait for the promise of the Father?

2. In what ways are the refiner's fire and launderer's soap fitting images for the cleansing and purifying work the Holy Spirit wants to do in our spiritual lives?

3. What does the Holy Spirit want to cleanse and purify in our hearts and lives?

4. In what ways does the work of the Holy Spirit in our lives go beyond forgiving us of past sins?

5. In what ways is your life a "living sacrifice" for God (Rom. 12:1-2)?

6. What is the difference between you consecrating yourself to God and God sanctifying you (1 Thess. 5:23-24)?

7. In what ways has the law of the Spirit "set you free from the law of sin and death" (Rom. 8:1-2)?

8. Why do you think people choose to continue to live in the bondage of disobedience when they could experience the freedom that comes from the Holy Spirit?

9. In what ways does your loyalty to the Spirit manifest itself in your daily life?

10. What encouragement do you receive from thinking of the Holy Spirit as the Spirit of Christ?

NINE

Gifts and Fruit

There is one body and one Spirit, just as you were called to one hope when you were called; one Lord, one faith, one baptism; one God and Father of all, who is over all and through all and in all.

—Ephesians 4:4-6

Every good gift is from God, and is given to man by the Holy Ghost. By nature there is in us no good thing; and there can be none, but so far as it is wrought in us by that good Spirit.

—John Wesley[1]

The Evidence

We live in a world that demands evidence. Everybody from courtroom lawyers to children on the playground frequently declare, "Show me the evidence." The previous chapter of this book, titled "Radical Transformation," claimed that the infilling with the Holy Spirit transformed the lives of Jesus's followers. So where do we see evidence of that radical transformation? The books of the New Testament following the Gospels offer numerous examples of the Holy Spirit transforming the lives of Jesus's followers.

Peter

Consider Peter, for example. Peter led the way in professing allegiance to Jesus regardless of the circumstances

---

1. Wesley, "Farther Appeal to Men," part 1, in *Works of John Wesley*, 8:106.

that might come his way. He declared, "I will lay down my life for you" (John 13:37). He did not believe Jesus when he responded, "Will you really lay down your life for me? Very truly I tell you, before the rooster crows, you will disown me three times!" (v. 38). Peter could not even begin to process such a ridiculous claim. Yet in the hours following Jesus's arrest and trial, Peter did exactly that.

The days following the crucifixion of Jesus found the disciples hiding from the Jewish religious leaders, fearful for their lives. "On the evening of that first day of the week, when the disciples were together, with the doors locked for fear of the Jewish leaders, Jesus came and stood among them and said, 'Peace be with you!'" (20:19). Jesus knew how fear gripped their hearts. That is why, as is so often the case with God's messengers, Jesus greeted them with words to bring peace to their hearts.

You might think that seeing their Lord alive and well would give the disciples courage to leave their locked doors behind and declare the resurrection of Jesus, but not so. The next week found them still hiding behind those same locked doors. Jesus appeared to them again in their safe room and again greeted them with words to bring peace to their hearts. "A week later his disciples were in the house again, and Thomas was with them. Though the doors were locked, Jesus came and stood among them and said, 'Peace be with you!'" (v. 26). These fearful disciples failed to accept the challenge to declare to the world, "He is risen; Jesus is Lord!" No profiles in courage with this group of disciples.

Yet something dramatic happened to Jesus's disciples. The day of Pentecost finds the disciples publicly speaking on the streets of Jerusalem to everyone who would listen to their message about the resurrected Jesus. The Jewish religious leaders, whom the disciples feared a few days prior, could now hear for themselves the incredible message about the risen Lord. Only the transforming power of the Holy Spirit could have changed the disciples so radically.

The disciples' boldness did not end following Pentecost. Peter and the other disciples returned to the streets of Jerusalem day after day preaching about Jesus and the resurrection of the dead (Acts 3–4). Then the event they had once feared the most happened to them: the religious leaders had them arrested and brought before the Sanhedrin. The Acts account does not leave us guessing about the source of their bold testimony: "Then Peter, filled with the Holy Spirit, said to them . . ." (4:8). I love the response of the Jewish leaders following Peter's powerful testimony. "When they saw the courage of Peter and John and realized that they were unschooled, ordinary men, they were astonished and they took note that these men had been with Jesus" (v. 13). The threats against the Spirit-empowered disciples fell on deaf ears as they testified, "We cannot help speaking about what we have seen and heard" (v. 20).

Saul

Leaders in the early church met stiff opposition from the religious establishment of the day. Sometimes the threats came from a body of leaders, like the Sanhedrin. At other times, threats came from individuals determined to silence the witness of the Spirit-filled disciples of Jesus. One of the most notorious persecutors of Christians watched with the crowd as members of the Sanhedrin stoned Stephen, the first Christian martyr (Acts 7:54–8:1). Truth is certainly stranger than fiction when we mention Saul's name. No one in the early church would have imagined that God could change Saul's heart from murderous persecutor to tireless disciple of Jesus. His "murderous threats against the Lord's disciples" (9:1) ended the day he met the risen Lord on the road to Damascus.

The account of Saul's conversion from persecutor to disciple of Jesus (vv. 1-18) testifies to more than a midlife crisis or a decision to turn over a new leaf. Jesus encountered Saul in a miraculous way that reoriented Saul's faith, beliefs, and mission in life. God used disciples in the early church, such as Ananias, to validate the transforming work of the Holy Spirit in his life (vv. 10-19). Verse 17 specifically mentions the infilling with the Holy Spirit. The remaining chapters in the book of Acts along with Paul's Epistles detail the powerful ministry Saul, later called Paul, conducted across the Roman Empire through the transforming power of the Holy Spirit.

The Early Church

Peter and Paul led the early Christian church in the days and years following Pentecost. Most enthusiastic religious movements lose the fire with which they started as the years mount. Not so with the early church. The proclamation of Jesus became the road map for the way the gospel message spread following Pentecost: "But you will receive power when the Holy Spirit comes on you; and you will be my witnesses in Jerusalem, and in all Judea and Samaria, and to the ends of the earth" (Acts 1:8). They witnessed first in Jerusalem, then on to Judea and Samaria, and then to the rest of the world.

A couple of amazing numbers appear in the growth records of the early church. We know that about three thousand individuals converted to the Christian faith following Peter's Pentecost sermon. Acts 4:4 increases the number of converts to about five thousand men. Records of that day tended to account for heads of households, as with the feeding of the five thousand men (John 6:1-13). If that is the case in the Acts account, then the Christian church very quickly made converts in five thousand households.

The record of the church's expansion highlighted the increasing number of disciples as the gospel crossed national and language barriers (Acts 6:1). Acts 6:7 recounts, "So the word of God spread. The number of disciples in Jeru-

The Spirit gives every believer gifts to exercise in the community of faith and witness to the world. The Spirit gives gifts to promote unity within the body of Christ.

salem increased rapidly." The missionary journeys of Paul, Barnabas, Silas, and others assisted the gospel in spreading across the entire Roman Empire. Acts 12:24 summarized it well, "But the word of God continued to spread and flourish." The secret to the growth and expansion of the gospel message remained the same throughout this era of church history. "Then Saul, who was also called Paul, filled with the Holy Spirit . . ." (13:9). Yes, the radical transformation of Christ's disciples with the infilling of the Holy Spirit led to the gospel's success throughout the Roman Empire.

The Gift Becomes the Giver of Gifts

Jesus gave his disciples final instructions in the upper room on their last full evening together before his arrest (John 14–16). He promised them an incredible gift following his return to the Father: the Holy Spirit. Following their wait together in the upper room, the Holy Spirit filled them on the day of Pentecost (Acts 2:1-4). This incredible gift of God's presence not only filled them and "purified their hearts by faith" (15:8-9) but also gave them gifts for ministry within the community of faith.

The Holy Spirit has continued to empower believers in the Christian church for the past two thousand years. He works in the lives of believers today just as he did in the early days of the Christian church. That includes you; the power of the Holy Spirit at work in your life gives you everything you need to grow in your faith and witness for Christ. His presence at work in your life assures that you are a child of God. "If anyone does not have the Spirit of Christ, they do not belong to Christ" (Rom. 8:9). The Spirit gives every believer gifts to exercise in the community of faith and witness to the world. The Spirit gives gifts to promote unity within the body of Christ. Paul admonished the Ephesians, "Make every effort to keep the unity of the Spirit through the bond of peace" (Eph. 4:3). Paul went on to describe that unity: "There is one body and one Spirit, just as you were called to one hope when you were called; one Lord, one faith, one baptism; one God and Father of all, who is over all and through all and in all" (vv. 4-6).

Scripture admonishes us to keep several perspectives in mind as we think about the gifts of the Spirit. For example,

- All gifts of the Spirit come from the same Holy Spirit, who indwells believers.
- The Holy Spirit decides which gifts are needed within the Christian community and then grants them accordingly.
- Some believers exercise a particular gift for a lifetime; others, for a limited period of time.
- No believer possesses all the gifts of the Spirit, but everyone has at least one gift.
- The gifts of the Spirit are for the benefit of the entire body of believers and not for individual benefit or carnal desire.
- A believer's gift(s) may be a special endowment of the Spirit, or they may be talents and abilities the believer already possesses that the Spirit may nurture.[2]
- God gives believers gifts of the Spirit "so that the purposes of Christ can be fulfilled through the church's ministry under the Spirit's leadership."[3]
- These gifts are "Christ's gifts to the church, administered by the Holy Spirit."[4]

---

2. Carter, *Person and Ministry*, 270-71.
3. Al Truesdale, ed., *Global Wesleyan Dictionary of Theology* (Kansas City: Beacon Hill Press of Kansas City, 2013), 213.
4. Ibid.

- Categories for these gifts include Spirit ministries within corporate worship, deeds of service, specific ministries or gifts, and activities.
- The exercise of spiritual gifts must be well ordered.
- All gifts of the Spirit are "necessary for the well-being of the church, no gift must be despised or unduly elevated."[5]
- "Diversity of gifts and unity of spirit are equally indispensable."[6]
- These gifts of the Spirit function correctly only when exercised within the body of Christ; "apart from the collective body . . . , individual members exist as dissected, grotesque, dead, and worthless body parts."[7]

The following list of gifts of the Spirit within the community of faith is descriptive of the many functions at work as believers minister to one another. The following list is random and suggestive, not exhaustive.

1. *Apostles.* They were eyewitnesses to the incarnation of Jesus Christ, who called them into service and commissioned them to serve as his ambassadors. Jesus named twelve apostles for his earthly ministry, but Paul broadened the definition to include himself as one Jesus commissioned later.
2. *Prophets.* They were messengers called by God to proclaim God's will and plan to his people. They were primarily concerned with representing God faithfully, not winning popularity with listeners. Hence they were usually ignored or persecuted.

---

5. Robert D. Branson, ed., *Global Wesleyan Encyclopedia of Biblical Theology* (Kansas City: Foundry, 2020), 145.
6. Ibid.
7. William M. Greathouse with George Lyons, *Romans 9–16*, New Beacon Bible Commentary (Kansas City: Beacon Hill Press of Kansas City, 2008), 147.

3. *Evangelists.* They were effective ministers of the good news about salvation in Jesus Christ. They often shared the gospel with people who had never heard it before. The term is only found in Acts 21:8, Ephesians 4:11, and 2 Timothy 4:5.
4. *Pastors.* They were the shepherds of the flock of God's people; they served the people "with nurture, care, counsel, and protection from false teachers."[8] Other titles include overseers, bishops, and elders.
5. *Teachers.* They were those who ministered by instructing believers in the community of faith about the doctrines and practices of the Christian church.[9]
6. *Service.* This gift, also translated "ministry," refers to a variety of functions within the community related to practical roles such as entertaining individuals at mealtime, distributing food, serving tables, cleaning after a worship service or fellowship event, making repairs to the church building, and assisting the poor.
7. *Encouragement.* This gift is the "God-given capacity to empathize with others and to motivate them to perseverance."[10] It includes activities such as pleading, urging, and exhorting others to live for the Lord. It urges believers to spur one another on to live a life of faithfulness as a believer by conversation and example.
8. *Giving.* This gift refers to sharing financial and material resources and using spiritual gifts to share the gospel message. When referencing financial

---
8. Lyons, Smith, and Lyons-Pardue, *Ephesians, Colossians, Philemon*, 151.
9. The first five gifts on this list may be found in Eph. 4:11-13.
10. Greathouse with Lyons, *Romans 9–16*, 151.

and material resources, they should be shared with generosity. When referencing spiritual gifts and the gospel message, they should be shared with sincerity.[11]

9. *Leadership.* This gift gives a believer the ability to stand in front of a group and give direction, both in word and by example. The believer with the gift of leadership should use it with eagerness, zeal, and diligence. The Spirit may give this gift to individuals elected to church offices, or it may also be given to any believer who takes on a leadership task for a particular situation.[12]

10. *Mercy.* A believer exercises this gift by taking care of sick people, assisting the poor and homeless, and ministering to old and disabled individuals. The work is done with cheerfulness, considering the opportunity as a privilege and not a burden. The one who offers mercy as a spiritual gift shares with others what has been received from God (2 Cor. 1:3-4).[13]

11. *Wisdom.* This gift of the Spirit enables a believer to have the unusual ability to explain the gospel message in a way that leads others to accept Christ as personal Savior. The Spirit gives the believer with this gift helpful insights from both reasoned thought and personal experience to share the gospel simply and persuasively.

12. *Knowledge.* The Holy Spirit guides the education and thinking processes of the believer with this gift, granting the ability to analyze a variety of Scripture passages, find appropriate illustrations,

---

11. Ibid.
12. Ibid.
13. Ibid. Gifts six through ten may be found in Rom. 12:6-8.

and use words that answer people's questions about God's plan of salvation and ways to live holy and righteously as believers in this world.
13. *Faith*. This spiritual gift provides a believer with the supernatural ability to trust the promises of Scripture and believe that God is working in situations that have no apparent evidence. It offers a divinely given hope and assurance of God's providence in the darkest night of the deepest valley. It sees into the future and grabs hold of God's answers to prayer.
14. *Healing*. The Holy Spirit grants a believer or a community of faith the ability to offer a prayer of faith for the healing of the sick. God may choose to answer this prayer with a miraculous divine touch or more naturally through medical science. Both answers come from the healing hand of God.[14]
15. *Miraculous Powers*. This spiritual gift gives a believer the ability to be a channel for God to use to accomplish answers to prayer that speed up natural processes, bring circumstances together in unusual ways, or defy human ability to explain. The exercise of this gift does not intend to impress or amaze others but to draw people's attention to the miracle-working hand of God intervening in our world.
16. *Discernment*. A believer with this spiritual gift has the ability to see and hear with eyes of faith and determine what is true or false in the lives of individuals as well as in what they say. This individual can quickly test a person's spirit and decide whether it is in harmony with God or not (1 John 4:1).

---

14. *Manual*, art. 14.

17. *Languages.* The Holy Spirit gifts certain believers with an unusual knack for learning another language. These individuals quickly learn the vocabulary, syntax, and rules of the language along with the idioms, voice inflections, and pronunciations necessary to converse naturally. This gift is especially useful for missionaries and other believers called by God to minister in cross-cultural settings.

18. *Interpretation of Languages.* This spiritual gift grants a believer the ability to interpret the spoken message or translate the written message of someone communicating with individuals who do not speak or read the original language. This gift is especially useful to assist those who need interpretation or translation to enable them to declare or write the gospel message.[15]

The gifts of the Spirit include more divine abilities than are contained in the above list. For example, the Holy Spirit also empowers those who serve in administrative, pastoral, and teaching roles within the community of faith. This list simply offers several ministries to which the Lord calls believers to serve. Many books have been written giving extensive details about these and other gifts of the Spirit. You may wish to read them to learn more about these Spirit-enabled ministries within the community of faith. You may also take a spiritual gifts inventory to learn more about the gifts the Holy Spirit has given you and wishes to exercise through you. Your local church pastor can assist you in finding and taking one of these inventories. Then you should get involved in the ministries of your church that benefit from your gifting. God often works through members of the community of faith to affirm the gifts and

---

15. Gifts eleven through eighteen may be found in 1 Cor. 12:7-11, 28-30.

The growth and maturation
of fruit takes time,
and some fruits
take longer to mature
than others.

graces they see in your life as you bless and minister to others. Listen to their encouragement. Listen also for the voice of the Holy Spirit confirming to your spirit the roles to which he is calling you. And remember the message Paul sent to a friend, "See to it that you complete the ministry you have received in the Lord" (Col. 4:17).

The Fruit of the Spirit

We turn our attention from the gifts of the Holy Spirit to the fruit of the Holy Spirit. The two categories differ in significant ways. First, notice that the word "gifts" appears in the plural. The list in the previous section offers stand-alone gifts that the Spirit grants to believers. The gifting can come in the form of a single ability or a combination of abilities for ministry within the community of faith. The word "fruit," on the other hand, appears in the singular. The nine virtues listed below function together in their various manifestations to form the fruit of the Christian life. Second, the Holy Spirit may give a believer one, two, or even three gifts for ministry. The Holy Spirit desires to produce fruit in the life of the believer that evidences itself in all of the nine virtues listed below. Third, we should not ask the Holy Spirit for one particular gift any more than we would ask a friend to buy us a certain gift. We should pray, on the other hand, for the Holy Spirit to develop each of the virtues in the list below in our lives as we grow in grace. Fourth, just as a gift is received in a moment of time, the Holy Spirit often grants us certain ministry abilities that become effective immediately. The growth and maturation of fruit takes time, and some fruits take longer to mature than others. For example, a tomato plant yields ripened red tomatoes in a matter of weeks; a pecan tree will not produce its first crop of nuts for several years.

With these clarifications in mind, we will now turn our attention to the various manifestations of the fruit of the Holy Spirit.

1. *Love.* This first virtue does not appear as simply one among many fruits of the Holy Spirit. It appears first because it is most important. Paul said in Galatians 5:6, "The only thing that counts is faith expressing itself through love." Without love, nothing else matters. Scripture speaks here not of an emotional, romantic, or familial love but of a divinely inspired love that flows from the heart of God. This love is not natural to us; it comes from above and causes us to act in ways that are not natural human actions or reactions. Our Spirit-inspired love comes to us as a gift from God and flows back to God and out to others as a supernatural response to God's unconditional love for us. Jesus summarized all Old Testament law with this command: "'Hear, O Israel: The Lord our God, the Lord is one. Love the Lord your God with all your heart and with all your soul and with all your mind and with all your strength.' . . . 'Love your neighbor as yourself'" (Mark 12:29-31). Paul described love well when he wrote, "Love is patient, love is kind. It does not envy, it does not boast, it is not proud. It does not dishonor others, it is not self-seeking, it is not easily angered, it keeps no record of wrongs. Love does not delight in evil but rejoices with the truth. It always protects, always trusts, always hopes, always perseveres" (1 Cor. 13:4-7).

2. *Joy.* Paul loved to talk about joy. In fact, he mentioned it 50 of the 133 times it is referenced in the entire New Testament. Christian joy does not result from favorable experiences or circumstances in life. It is not an emotion; it is a reasoned choice to value

all of life with delight at God's presence and work in a believer's life and in the world. It flows from a right relationship with God and an anticipation of all that awaits believers as they live in the power of the Holy Spirit.

3. *Peace.* "Peace is a state of well-being that is God's gift to people who love faithfully within his covenant."[16] It is a state of being that results from living life with the indwelling presence of the Holy Spirit. It does not look to the circumstances of life, money in the bank, material possessions, or any other indicator so valued by the world. It offers the inner awareness that all is well because God is always near. From Bible days until today, the Hebrew people greet one another with "Shalom" (peace), which "expresses an implicit prayer, 'May you be well. May you have the physical and spiritual resources you need. May you enjoy the blessings of the age to come.'"[17]

4. *Forbearance.* This Christian virtue may be translated patience or steadfastness. In the biblical context it means simply "to delay wrath." Its practice makes a person long-tempered, not short-tempered. It forgives others over and over, even when not asked to do so. It gives people the benefit of doubt that we would want them to give us. "When we practice patience, we see others less for what they are now, than for what they could be by the grace of God."[18]

5. *Kindness.* This "is grace expressed in human relations, by being helpful when anger might be the

---

16. George Lyons, *Galatians*, New Beacon Bible Commentary (Kansas City: Beacon Hill Press of Kansas City, 2012), 350.
17. Ibid.
18. Ibid., 351.

expected, natural response."[19] Paul is the only New Testament author to use this word. He often used it to describe God, as in "the riches of his [God's] kindness, forbearance, and patience, not realizing that God's kindness is intended to lead you to repentance" (Rom. 2:4).

6. *Goodness.* This virtue is a synonym of the previous one. It "describes loving actions that contribute to the well-being, building-up, and salvation of others."[20] The Old Testament frequently stated that God's goodness flows from his love (1 Chron. 16:34; 2 Chron. 5:13; Ezra 3:11). Jesus said that only God can completely exhibit goodness (Matt. 19:17; Mark 10:18; Luke 18:19). However, the infilling of the Holy Spirit in the lives of believers enables them to express goodness.

7. *Faithfulness.* Old Testament teachers of the law defined this virtue as obeying the law of Moses. The New Testament, on the other hand, regarded it as "essentially a lifestyle of sustained, obedient trustworthiness and loyalty to God and others."[21] This virtue does not result from one or two responses but from the long, consistent, obedient response to God over a lifetime.

8. *Gentleness.* This virtue exhibits itself when a believer does not think too highly of himself or herself. It speaks to a person's humility and meekness. It "involves respecting all people as worthy creatures of God, not as means to selfish ends."[22] Christ exhibited this virtue perfectly. The infilling of the

---

19. Ibid.
20. Ibid., 351-52.
21. Ibid., 352.
22. Ibid., 353.

Holy Spirit allows believers to display this Christ-like response as a divinely produced fruit.

9. *Self-Control.* The name of this virtue is actually an oxymoron. Use of the word "self" might seem to imply that an individual can control behavior, reactions, attitudes, and feelings through self-effort. Human achievement can never master all that should be controlled in the experiences of life. This virtue is actually the fruit of the infilling of the Holy Spirit. Believers need divine assistance in exercising positive self-discipline. This virtue is never mentioned in the Gospels but appears in Paul's writings as a lofty goal within Greek philosophy that can only be realized through the power of God.

Paul ended this list of spiritual fruit by saying, "Against such things there is no law" (Gal. 5:23). By that he meant the same thing Jesus meant in the Sermon on the Mount when comparing his commands with the Ten Commandments. That is, these virtues exceed the requirements of the law. We should not think of these virtues as "extra credit" that we tried to earn to boost our grade. We cannot produce these fruits by striving for them. They flourish in our lives as a by-product of the infilling with the Holy Spirit. As Paul said, "For this reason, since the day we heard about you, we have not stopped praying for you. We continually ask God to fill you with the knowledge of his will through all the wisdom and understanding that the Spirit gives, so that you may live a life worthy of the Lord and please him in every way: bearing fruit in every good work, growing in the knowledge of God" (Col. 1:9-10).

Focus on You

Much of this book has focused attention on the person and work of the Holy Spirit in the Old Testament, the incarnation of Jesus, and the early church. This chapter focuses attention on your life and work within the community of faith as well as your influence on family members, coworkers, and neighbors. The gifts and fruits of the Spirit offer you everything you need to effectively witness for Christ as well as live a Christlike life. We must always use the gifts and fruits of the Spirit humbly as we remember the words of Paul: "For it is by grace you have been saved, through faith—and this is not from yourselves, it is the gift of God—not by works, so that no one can boast" (Eph. 2:8-9).

Words to Describe the Holy Spirit

1. Gift Giver
2. Fruit Producer

Questions for Reflection

1. How would you describe to a friend the radical difference the Holy Spirit made in Peter's life at Pentecost?

2. In what way was the work of the Holy Spirit in Saul's life different from the way it was in Peter's life?

3. How did the Holy Spirit enable early church believers to expand the Christian church from Jerusalem to the entire Roman Empire?

4. What new insight did you learn as you read about the different perspectives the Bible uses to explain the gifts of the Spirit?

5. Give the names of individuals in your community of faith who exhibit one or more of the gifts of the Spirit and tell which gifts you see in them.

6. Which gifts of the Spirit do you see in your own life?

7. How might God use you more effectively in ministering to others with the gift(s) the Spirit has given you?

8. Which manifestations of the fruit of the Spirit do you see in your own life?

9. Which manifestations of the fruit of the Spirit might God want to improve in your life?

10. What are some of the by-products of the infilling of the Holy Spirit in your life?

TEN

Best Friend Forever

When Solomon finished praying, fire came down from heaven and consumed the burnt offering and the sacrifices, and the glory of the LORD filled the temple.

—2 Chronicles 7:1

The heart that is filled with an holy awe and reverence of the divine glory, to which God manifests his greatness, and (which is no less his glory) his goodness, is thereby owned as a living temple.

—John Wesley[1]

His Presence

Contemplating memories of the Holy Spirit's presence in my life brings two experiences to mind. The first occurred every summer on the Friday morning of youth camp. A flood of images always hit me just before we pulled out of the parking lot for the long ride home: making new friends in the cabin, late-night talks until the cabin counselor quieted us down, playing practical jokes on each other, baseball games, meals in the mess hall, Bible classes, morning and evening worship services, and prayer times. I got the same pit in my stomach on each of these Friday mornings; I wanted more than anything to stay at camp. I didn't want to return home to my daily routine.

---

1. Wesley, *Explanatory Notes upon the Old Testament*, 2:1356 (comment on 2 Chron. 7:1).

As I grew older, I analyzed what prompted the strong desire to linger just a little longer at the campground. I wasn't going to miss the weather; it was always too hot and humid. I wasn't going to miss the mess-hall meals; they weren't anything to photograph and paste in a photo album. I wasn't going to miss the busy schedule; camp directors kept us going from early morning to late night. I realized I would miss my friends. But most of all, I didn't want to leave because I had just spent a week experiencing the presence of God in powerful ways. I didn't want to lose that sense of his presence. Those Friday mornings on the last day of church camp represented a mountaintop spiritual experience second to none in my life.

The other experience occurred during fall and spring revival services at the Christian university I attended. The student body, along with laypeople from the local church, gathered every morning for chapel services and every evening for evangelistic services. The music and sermons were always great, but they did not stand out for special recognition. What I remember most was what happened at the close of many of those services. The minister always invited people to come to the prayer altar and pray if they felt God calling. Several students and lay members usually came and prayed at the altar and then returned to their seats.

Then, with music playing softly in the background, everyone would sit in dead silence. Nobody would move. Some prayed quietly to themselves. Some looked at the light shining through the stained-glass windows at the front of the sanctuary. Others just sat quietly soaking in the moment. Why did everyone sit in silence? Because we felt the presence of God in such a tangible way that we didn't want to leave. We lingered for a long time at this mountaintop spiritual experience.

Friday morning of summer youth camp and college revival services—both experiences captured a brief glimpse of the work of the Holy Spirit bringing the presence of God to us in undeniable ways. I am not sure about many things in this uncertain world; I am sure that a sense of God's presence offers one of the most meaningful experiences of life.

Three More Descriptive Words

We have offered a variety of words in this book to describe the Holy Spirit. At the end of this chapter we have included a list of some of these words. As we close this study, here are three more words to add to the list.

1. *Seal.* In Bible times a ruling monarch wore a signet ring. After making an official decree, the monarch would roll up the parchment paper, drip warm candle wax at the rolled seam, and then press the ring into the warm wax. This created a seal for the document that represented the authority of the monarch. In this same way, the Holy Spirit impresses his signet ring on the warm wax of our soul in a moment. Paul summarized it in this way: "And you also were included in Christ when you heard the message of truth, the gospel of your salvation. When you believed, you were marked in him with a seal, the promised Holy Spirit" (Eph. 1:13).

2. *Deposit.* Merchants will often let you place a deposit on an item that interests you to prevent anyone else from buying it for a specified time. A deposit is a promise a person makes that he or she will close the deal soon. Paul had that image in mind when he wrote that God "set his seal of ownership on us, and put his Spirit in our hearts as a deposit, guaranteeing what is to come" (2 Cor. 1:22). Thus the Holy Spirit lives within us as a guarantee that our salvation is secure in Christ Jesus. We will make it safely to heaven someday.

3. *Incomprehensible.* That does not mean we can't know anything about the Holy Spirit; it means we can't know everything about him. That is, we will never master him with our limited human understanding. But we can love him, live in fellowship with him, and allow him to work through us as he infills our hearts and lives. We can be sure of that even as we acknowledge our limited understanding.

I Don't Understand

I have had many conversations with individuals who told me they could never become Christians, because Christianity has too many beliefs that are difficult to understand. I get their reservation but find their argument weak. Think for a minute about the conveniences we use daily that defy our understanding. The list is nearly endless.

For example, my wife and I were sitting in a jumbo jet at the end of the runway in Buenos Aires one night waiting for clearance to take off. With all of the lights in the cabin turned off and a soft flicker of a runway marker shining through our window, we sat in silence except for the hum of the idling jet engines. The pilot decided to pass the time by giving us a few fun facts about our aircraft and the trip for the evening. He said 390 passengers were on board that night. The weight of the aircraft with passengers, crew, and luggage was just under 750,000 pounds. Our plane could go eleven thousand nautical miles on full tanks of fuel, but our flight to Miami was a mere forty-four hundred miles. He said the twin engines would push through two million cubic feet of air per minute on takeoff. At that point my brain hit an overload and shut down. I could no longer process his information.

The facts and figures of modern aviation boggle my mind. However, I have enough faith in the design team of the aircraft, the engineers who tested each component, the

God's self-revelation gives us more than random facts scattered throughout the Bible; it offers us a way of living daily in close personal relationship with God.

factory employees who assembled the various aircraft parts, along with the pilots and crew members on board our planes, that I trust my life, along with the lives of my family members, into their care. So do millions of other people every day.

Here is another mystery. As I continued to sit in silence that night on the plane, the cell phone in my pocket vibrated that I had a text message. I know what you are thinking; my cell phone should have been in airplane mode by that time. I forgot. I checked the text message; it was from my friend telling me that he would be praying for us on our journey home. So explain to me how my friend's text traveled from Kansas to my phone in Buenos Aires in only a few seconds. I positively cannot grasp that technology, but I use it every day anyway.

Limited understanding of divine realities should never hinder our spiritual journey. God's self-revelation gives us more than random facts scattered throughout the Bible; it offers us a way of living daily in close personal relationship with God. God created us for relationship with himself. We will never be satisfied or fulfilled in life until we enjoy that relationship.

Focused Attention

I have attempted in this book to focus your attention on the life and ministry of the Holy Spirit in the self-revelation of God to us and in revealing to us God's plan for our eternal salvation. Here are the topics we have considered together:

1. We began by saying the purpose of the Bible and theological study must go beyond mastering a body of knowledge about God. We invest in learning as much as we can about the Holy Spirit because we want to know him more personally,

surrender to him more completely, and be filled with his presence more fully.
2. The Holy Spirit is the third person of the Trinity. The Bible does not use the word "trinity" but offers examples of one God in three persons, particularly in the baptism of Jesus and the Great Commission (Matt. 28:19-20).
3. The Holy Spirit played an essential role in the creation of everything and in making us living souls. Following creation, the Spirit of God has worked in providential ways to maintain all that God created. The Holy Spirit has been actively involved in the re-creation of humanity from the garden fall until today.
4. Both the old and new covenants between God and humanity provided ways for the Holy Spirit to work with individual believers. In old-covenant days, the Spirit worked primarily *with* believers. In the new covenant, which we enjoy in the church age, the Spirit works primarily *in* believers.
5. The Holy Spirit worked quietly, often behind the scenes, throughout the entire Old Testament preparing the way for the coming Messiah, who would save his people from their sins and restore the relationship between God and humanity.
6. The Holy Spirit worked directly in the life, ministry, teaching, death, resurrection, and ascension of Jesus Christ. Not only do we benefit from the gift of salvation in Christ because of the work of the Spirit, but we also learn from Christ's example about ways the Holy Spirit wants to work in our lives.
7. Much of what we know about the Holy Spirit comes from Jesus's last extended conversation with his disciples in the upper room following the Last Supper (John 14–16). He carefully explained to

his disciples the work the Holy Spirit would do in their hearts and lives as well as in spreading the gospel message after Jesus returned to the Father.
8. In order for believers to be formed into the image of Christ, they need a radical transformation of their inner nature, with the Spirit purifying their hearts by faith. Further, they need the empowerment that comes with the infilling of the Holy Spirit.
9. The Holy Spirit works in the lives of believers following regeneration and entire sanctification by giving them gifts of the Spirit for ministry within the body of Christ and the fruit of the Spirit as they live their lives in the power of the Spirit.
10. The Holy Spirit continues to mature believers in the Christian faith as they grow in grace until they go to live in the uninterrupted presence of God forever. Everything we have said in this book has resulted from this statement of faith:

> We believe in the Holy Spirit, the Third Person of the Triune Godhead, that He is ever present and efficiently active in and with the Church of Christ, convincing the world of sin, regenerating those who repent and believe, sanctifying believers, and guiding into all truth as it is in Jesus.[2]

BFF

I have attempted in this book to expand our understanding of the Holy Spirit with all of the reverence and awe due him as third person of the Trinity. At the same time, I did not want to present the Almighty Sovereign of the universe as distant and disconnected from humanity,

---

2. *Manual*, art. 3.

which he created in his image. I hope I have been able to maintain that balance. I am sensitive to this perspective because of a special speaker I heard as a university student. The pastor invited a noteworthy sports figure of the day to speak to the students who attended the college church. The athlete gave his testimony about his conversion to Christ and offered insights into his spiritual journey. Throughout his presentation he used a phrase that I found somewhat disrespectful: "Me and JC are best buds." I know he was trying to relate to us college students. However, I'm not sure I want to refer to my Lord and Savior as JC.

I think it is completely respectful and scriptural, on the other hand, to refer to God the Father through Jesus Christ the Son in the power of the Holy Spirit as our best friend. In Isaiah 41:8-9 God said, "But you, Israel, my servant, Jacob, whom I have chosen, you descendants of Abraham my friend, I took you from the ends of the earth, from its farthest corners I called you. I said, 'You are my servant'; I have chosen you and have not rejected you." Notice that God called Abraham his friend. I like that, friend of God.

If you are a believer, I am sure you know him as your best friend. And you will live in the place he has prepared for you (John 14:1-4) for all eternity—that is, forever. I want to leave you with this one last thought about the Holy Spirit, the Spirit of Christ. He is your best friend forever!

I want to close with this prayer for you:

For this reason I kneel before the Father, from whom every family in heaven and on earth derives its name. I pray that out of his glorious riches he may strengthen you with power through his Spirit in your inner being, so that Christ may dwell in your hearts through faith. And I pray that you, being rooted and established in love, may have power, together with all the Lord's holy people, to grasp how wide and long and high and deep is the love of Christ, and to know this love that surpasses knowledge—that you may be filled to the measure of all the fullness of God.

Now to him who is able to do immeasurably more than all we ask or imagine, according to his power that is at work within us, to him be glory in the church and in Christ Jesus throughout all generations, for ever and ever! Amen. (Eph. 3:14-21)

Words to Describe the Holy Spirit: Final List

Almighty	Truthful	Leader	Spirit of Christ
Sovereign	Faithful	Guide	Gift Giver
Creator	Persistent	Empowerer	Fruit Producer
Friend	Eternal	Fulfiller	Seal
Trinity	Re-creator	Anointer	Deposit
Omnipresent	Sustainer	Life Giving	Incomprehensible
Living	Spirit of the Lord	Advocate	Best Friend Forever
Holy	Empowering	Comforter	
Righteous	Indwelling	Defender	
Loving	Planner	Intercessor	
Omniscient	Enabler	Sanctifier	
Omnipotent	Preparer	Transformer	

Bibliography

The Book of Common Prayer. New York: Seabury Press, 1979.

Braaten, Laurie J., and Jim Edlin. *Nahum–Malachi*. New Beacon Bible Commentary. Kansas City: Beacon Hill Press of Kansas City, 2019.

Branson, Robert D., ed. *Global Wesleyan Encyclopedia of Biblical Theology*. Kansas City: Foundry, 2020.

Carter, Charles Webb. *The Person and Ministry of the Holy Spirit: A Wesleyan Perspective*. Grand Rapids: Baker, 1974.

Coleson, Joseph. *Genesis 1–11*. New Beacon Bible Commentary. Kansas City: Beacon Hill Press of Kansas City, 2012.

Greathouse, William M., with George Lyons. *Romans 9–16*. New Beacon Bible Commentary. Kansas City: Beacon Hill Press of Kansas City, 2008.

Holmes, Laura Sweat, and George Lyons. *John 1–12*. New Beacon Bible Commentary. Kansas City: Beacon Hill Press of Kansas City, 2020.

Joyce, G. C., "Deism." In vol. 4 of *Encyclopedia of Religion and Ethics*, edited by James Hastings. New York: Scribner, 1955.

Kelle, Brad E. *Ezekiel*. New Beacon Bible Commentary. Kansas City: Beacon Hill Press of Kansas City, 2013.

Lyons, George. *Galatians*. New Beacon Bible Commentary. Kansas City: Beacon Hill Press of Kansas City, 2012.

Lyons, George, and T. Scott Daniels. *John 13–21*. New Beacon Bible Commentary. Kansas City: Beacon Hill Press of Kansas City, 2020.

Lyons, George, Robert W. Smith, and Kara Lyons-Pardue. *Ephesians, Colossians, Philemon*. New Beacon Bible Commentary. Kansas City: Beacon Hill Press of Kansas City, 2019.

Manual, Church of the Nazarene, 2017–2021. Kansas City: Nazarene Publishing House, 2017.

"The Martyrdom of Polycarp." In *The Apostolic Fathers*. Translated by J. B. Lightfoot and J. R. Harmer. 2nd ed., edited by Michael W. Holmes. Grand Rapids: Baker, 1989.

Neale, David A. *Luke 1–9*. New Beacon Bible Commentary. Kansas City: Beacon Hill Press of Kansas City, 2011.

———. *Luke 9–24*. New Beacon Bible Commentary. Kansas City: Beacon Hill Press of Kansas City, 2013.

Tertullian. *Against Praxeas*. Translated by A. Souter. New York: Macmillan, 1920.

Thompson, Richard P. *Acts*. New Beacon Bible Commentary. Kansas City: Beacon Hill Press of Kansas City, 2015.

Truesdale, Al, ed. *Global Wesleyan Dictionary of Theology*. Kansas City: Beacon Hill Press of Kansas City, 2013.

Varughese, Alex, and Mitchel Modine. *Jeremiah 26–52*. New Beacon Bible Commentary. Kansas City: Beacon Hill Press of Kansas City, 2010.

Wesley, John. *Explanatory Notes upon the Old Testament*. 3 vols. Bristol, UK: William Pine, 1765. Repr., Salem, OH: Schmul, 1975.

———. *The Works of John Wesley*. 3rd ed., edited by Thomas Jackson. 14 vols. London: Wesleyan Methodist Book Room, 1872. Repr., Grand Rapids: Baker, 1979.

Lightning Source UK Ltd.
Milton Keynes UK
UKHW020621010223
416280UK00021B/310